When you leave the military, it's like jumping off a fast moving train. The train continues on without you as it moves at high speed down the track. At some point you jump off and are left wondering, "What am I going to do now, and whom will I turn to for help?" Michael Bluemling Jr.'s new self-help book will definitely help you answer these questions.

Lisa R. Taylor
CWDP Business Services and Community Relations Coordinator US Navy Spouse

I wish this book had been available when I was transitioning to the civilian sector. *Bridging the Gap from Soldier to Civilian* is written in clean, everyday language anyone can read and interpret. Highlighted text guides the reader's attention to calls-to-action. We all know life is full of uncertainty; this book does a great job of removing uncertainty during a major transition in our lives. Follow these simple suggestions, and your transition should go smoothly.

Mark Cosby
Chief Recycling Officer,
3 Dimensions Recycling, HM1 USN

The military does a wonderful job of conforming you to military life, training you while you're in and taking care of you along the way. But it doesn't train you to be a civilian or on how to transition back to being one. *Bridging the Gap from Soldier to Civilian: A Road Map to Success for Veterans* does just that. Thanks to Michael Bluemling Jr.'s self- help book, you too can find success as you transition from military life.

Edward N. Lazzari III
Staff Sergeant, US Army (Ret.)

Intelligent and insightful, *Bridging the Gap from Soldier to Civilian: A Road Map to Success for Veterans* enlightens veterans transitioning back into the public sector. Michael systematically covers all areas leading to your passion and purpose in life.

Charles Bright
USMC

I thought my military experience was all I needed to secure a well-paying job after I exited the army. How wrong I was. Until you get your degree, training, or certification, you will be qualified but not certified. The military gets you qualified. Unfortunately, qualified will not always get you the job. HOOAH!

> Jameo D. Pollock
> Staff Sergeant, US Army (Ret.)

Michael Bluemling's *Bridging the Gap from Soldier to Civilian* is a comprehensive guide for soldiers to transition from active duty to civilian life successfully. This book details step by step how to take your military skills to pave the way to a successful civilian career. It's a must for veterans to have this self-help book in their possession to assist in integrating the job market after military service.

> Allen Allison
> US Army Veteran and retired Compliance Officer

For any veteran struggling with transitioning back into the civilian world, *Bridging the Gap* provides a glass of cold water in a dry and discouraging desert filled with many challenges and obstacles. Michael not only captures the essence of this struggle but also provides a comprehensive list of thoughtful, encouraging, and pragmatic solutions.

> John Mahshie
> US Air Force Veteran
> Founder of Veterans Healing Farm

Bridging the Gap from Soldier to Civilian

A Road Map to Success for Veterans

Michael Bluemling Jr.

Book Publishers Network
P.O. Box 2256
Bothell • WA • 98041
Ph • 425-483-3040
www.bookpublishersnetwork.com

10 9 8 7 6 5 4 3 2 1

Printed in the United States of America

LCCN   2016933282
ISBN   978-1-940598-95-6

Editor: Julie Scandora
Cover Designer: Laura Zugzda
Book Designer: Melissa Vail Coffman

*This book is dedicated to all the brave men and women
who have served our country proudly and
protected the freedoms we enjoy today.*

Contents

Foreword by David A. Rababy. ix

Introduction xi

Phase 1: Expiration of Time and Service from the Military 1

    Chapter 1: Information and Data Collection 3

    Chapter 2: Getting all Personal Affairs in Order . . . 17

    Chapter 3: Medical Documentation Preparation . . . 29

Phase 2: Personal and Professional Growth as a Civilian . 43

    Chapter 4: Psychological Well-Being. 45

    Chapter 5: Education and Certification via the GI BILL . . 59

    Chapter 6: Creating Connections through Networking . . 73

    Chapter 7: Starting a Business as a Vetrepreneur . . . 87

    Chapter 8: Find Your Passion, Stay Dedicated,

        and Keep Climbing. 101

Conclusion 105

Acknowledgments 107

Veterans Resources List 109

About the Author. 115

Foreword

Serving in today's all-volunteer US military is a life-changing experience. Going from a civilian society, where every freedom is afforded to an individual and where individuality is embraced and encouraged, to an environment of teamwork, where completely different values are espoused, is not an easy transition. Putting others ahead of yourself is not something commonly found in our society, yet it is the cornerstone of military life. Once you have experienced this life-changing event, you become part of something bigger than yourself. You dedicate your very life to your country, your comrades, and often, total strangers. Your commonality is the uniform, the flag, the *esprit de corps* of knowing that you are all there for one sole purpose: to defend the nation "against all enemies, foreign and domestic."

Everyone who wears the uniform wears it temporarily. Sooner or later, we all must hang it up. This return to civilian life can be traumatic, regardless of whether you served three or thirty years. You were entrusted with ultimate killing machines, equipment worth millions of dollars, and people's lives. You lived in austere conditions, you endured extreme temperatures, you ate odd foods, and you survived. Being in the military is a lot like playing a team sport. You train, rehearse, and practice routinely in the event that you will get put into the game, except this game could end up costing your life. No one wants to practice all the time without testing one's mettle and facing one's greatest fears.

A combat veteran experiences things that are also life changing. A combat vet will see, smell, hear, taste, and experience things that are horrific. No normal person can experience combat and walk away from it without being affected in some fashion. Today's military takes the combat experience and puts time limits on it—usually six months to a year. During this period, you are living in an alternative universe, a universe where you are hyper-vigilant 24/7. Your survival skills become enhanced and sharpened to ensure that you make it back to the "real world" unharmed.

Once you return to the "real world," you find it different, or is it you who is different? Suddenly, crowds have an adverse impact upon you. Sudden movements or loud noises can cause a reflex that saved your life over there, but now it draws stares and whispers. Your family and friends treat you differently; they know you experienced life-changing events. Some don't want to talk about those events; others callously ask about every detail. Suddenly, you find yourself a stranger in your own land. How do you navigate your way home? The best way I have found is by learning from others just as you have learned methods of dealing with your new life. One person you can learn from is Michael Bluemling Jr.—a young man who has been there and done that and who provides a wealth of information in these pages to improve your quality of life as a veteran.

Semper Fidelis,
David A. Rababy
Lt. Col., USMC (ret.)

Introduction

Having the opportunity to serve in the United States Military is an honor and a privilege. Not everyone gets the opportunity to serve his or her country and to be a part of American history. Generations and generations of family members have given so much of themselves in order to protect our freedom and our way of life, both at home and abroad. Many patriots have also sacrificed their lives without the opportunity ever to say goodbye to the ones they love, which bring tears to my eyes.

A soldier's life is not an easy one, regardless of which branch of the service you are in. Being a part of the United States Army not only changed my life, but it has also allowed me to see the world from a new perspective. I see the strain that families are put through on constant deployments. I see how it is when you come back to your home of record or are discharged. I see the pain that lives on in the hearts and minds of those who lost someone they loved as their brother and sister on the battlefield. I see the obstacles we veterans face in becoming rehabilitated in a society that will never understand what we have endured in serving our country honorably.

The book you are about to read is written by someone who served his country for four years with one downrange KFOR deployment, was honorably discharged, and who has overcome so much to become the man he is today. I am that person. Besides my military service, I have lived through low-paying jobs, I have suffered through a painful divorce, I have struggled to go back to school to get my bachelor's and master's degrees while working full-time, I have started a business with very limited capital, I have lived through depression and anxiety, I have fought the Department of Veterans Affairs for years to get my disability rating adjusted, and I have also survived it all, thus far. Life is a struggle, but together we can adapt and overcome!

I want to take everything I have learned and pass it on to the next soldier about to experience his or her ETS (Expiration of Term of Service) from the military or to a veteran who is struggling to see the forest through the trees. One of the most powerful aspects of being a soldier or veteran is the camaraderie that exists between two people who have lived through similar circumstances. You spend five minutes with a fellow veteran, regardless of his or her background, and in most cases, it is as if you just met your new best friend. It is such an amazing feeling to know there are people in this world who understand you and know exactly where you are coming from during your time of need.

The truth is that we all need one another, regardless of where we served during our military service or what point of our lives we are at post-military. We cannot do it alone. We have to stick together, and we must help one another. Almost every veteran I know has had at least one veteran who has helped him in one way or another. I am another one of your friends, though we have never met. I care about your well-being and your life. I cannot sit back and watch as veterans turn to suicide because they feel all alone or abandoned. Every soldier's life matters! I pray that my book is a helpful resource to you and all veterans. I hope it allows you to move forward with a sense of urgency, knowing that you will succeed sooner rather than later.

Phase 1

★ ★ ★

Expiration of Time and Service from the Military

Chapter 1
Information and Data Collection

If I had known what I now know, my transition would have been a hell of a lot smoother. It was as if I was blind and was constantly bumping into every wall while trying to adapt as a civilian because of how uninformed I was. Looking back to when I was a twenty-two-year-old SGT in the United States Army discharging honorably, I thought I knew everything about life, when I actually knew absolutely nothing.

Being informed is the single most important aspect of making an intelligent decision for your life. As you are beginning to think about leaving the military, you must be aware of everything going on around you at a rapid pace. Your countdown to your last day of service may have begun months ago, but you have a critical job to do before you start to think about your life outside the military.

Your preparation begins now.

Ask yourself, "Who are my leaders, and who are the people around me who can help me in my transition? Are the soldiers around me focused on themselves, or do they actually care about my enlistment being over? Who can I go to for help, and where can I go for help?" These questions and many others probably are or will be running through your mind constantly as you develop a plan of action for where your life is going.

Many factors come into play when you are making a decision that will forever shape your future and your family's as well. You have to think through each step logically to find the balance you are searching for as a soon-to-be civilian again. Military life and civilian life are completely different experiences, and you need to have a mindset that no matter the obstacle, you will get through it successfully.

Following are seven steps you will need to follow to prepare yourself for returning to civilian life. Let's look at each one in detail.

7 Steps to Prepare Yourself for Your ETS

1. Talk to your family about your decision and the impacts of leaving the military.

2. Make up a list of goals for yourself.

3. Analyze your military skills to determine your best course of action.

4. Talk to your chain of command about life after the military.

5. Set up an appointment with a career adviser on base.

6. Contact a state veteran career adviser where you will be relocating.

7. Research and collect market data for the field you will be entering.

Step 1: Talk to Your Family about Your Decision and the Impacts of Leaving the Military

Deciding to leave the military at the end of your service commitment or at the end of a lustrous career can be the toughest period of your entire life. You may have just come off a recent deployment or could even be in a foreign country, which makes this period of your life extremely difficult and leaves you with hundreds of questions on your mind regarding what the future holds for you.

Before you attempt to sift through the entire process of collecting data and information about relocating or staying where you currently are stationed, you need to know what your family's expectations are. The key is deciding whether your ideas align with what your family thinks is best. This concern may not apply to everyone, but more likely than not, it applies to the majority.

> **A main point to consider is that your family has made many sacrifices over the years so you could accomplish everything you have in your career.**

Without the letters, support, love, and encouragement you received during your military service, you probably would not be where you are today. Your family members are probably your biggest supporters, so you need them to get from Point A to Point B, wherever that may be.

Ask your family questions and set up a clear line of communication well in advance of your ETS date. This is especially important because various circumstances can change a date or plan in the blink of an eye, so you need to be prepared as a team. Gathering as much information as possible about what others think about your leaving the military is very important, and it may save you from making one of the biggest mistakes of your life.

All the family values you learned in the military now need to be directly applied to your real family, whether they are currently living with you or are back home at your home of record. If you do not have a family to consult with, you can turn to friends or spiritual leaders for valuable support and guidance during this decision-making process that will alter your life forever.

Step 2: Make Up a List of Goals for Yourself

As you begin this process, you start to uncover more and more information, even at the earliest stages, that you never considered before. This information is great and will really have a positive impact for you down the road, once you have a plan of action that is well-thought-out and concise. One of the most important steps moving forward is to ask yourself the following two questions:

> **What do I want in my life personally and professionally? How am I going to get it?**

To answer these very important questions, sit down and write out a list of thoughts in a logical manner. It is a best practice to try to brainstorm and think outside the box in order to visualize where you see yourself in one to two years. You should also think about where you will be in five to ten years. The key is to look at not only the short-term but also the long-term, best-case scenario of what you see in your future. You can have fun with it and make your dreams as lofty as you can imagine because what you believe you can achieve, and you will in your every endeavor moving forward.

You will be pleasantly surprised by what you can come up with when you really think big. If you are thinking to yourself, *There is no way I can do this or I could do that,* ask yourself, "Why can't I do it?" The answer is you can. If you want something bad enough, in most cases you can get it. It may not be easy, but the end result is what you should focus on. Now that you have put a lot of thought into where you see yourself, it is time to analyze your results and set goals for getting there.

Setting goals is the fun part, because after determining your deepest thoughts and ambitions, you now get to turn them into reality. The process of taking your thoughts and making them into actions is what separates the soldier who has a plan from the soldier who is not sure what to do. You do not want to leave the military without a plan and then try to create a plan after the fact. There is a chance you could pull it off by winging it, but more times than not, it will take years to recover from such a mistake.

As you learned in the military, "time on target" is crucial to your transition. It is critical for you to set realistic goals that are professionally in line with your future career path and that align with your personal life. You are the steam to your engine, and loading up on reliable information about your prospective future and analyzing whether it is a good fit for you will make the difference between happiness and, in some cases, failure. Failure is not an option. Believe that you will succeed in all your future endeavors!

Step 3: Analyze Your Military Skills to Determine Your Best Course of Action

One area to look at before you get too wrapped up in exactly what you want to do post-military employment is how the skills you gained in the military can be applied in the civilian sector. This element is very important to consider. For example, if you are in the medical field in the military and want to start a business, do you have the entrepreneurial skills necessary to do so, or do you need more training or education first? You need to ask yourself these types of questions before you start putting an extensive amount of time and energy into an idea that may not be feasible at the moment.

A few specific areas of your military service record should be looked at to determine the validity of your skills and how they might or might not transfer into the private sector. Here are some points to consider:

- The training or skills you think will be transferable may not be.
- The skills necessary to enter a field you may have been trained in by the military may not specifically transfer outside the military.
- Some of the certificates you earned in the military may not automatically transfer or be recognized.

For these reasons, you must do some direct research and some investigating to determine how your military skills will transfer over and whether you need to take any additional courses or be recertified.

Once you find out what skills and certificates are applicable, you can start to map out a more definite plan for how you are going to start attacking the workforce you are about to enter with millions of other applicants across the United States. The quicker you identify your strengths and weaknesses, the quicker you can begin to strengthen your resume.

You are about to be in for the fight of your life, but if you are properly prepared, everything will be easier in the long run.

Finally, your military skills can be looked at two different ways. They can be looked at as a superior asset to a corporation, or they can be looked at as a detriment because your skills may be unrecognizable as far as actionable results in the private sector. This is why you have to be prepared to overcome any and all objections from an employer who may be hesitant to acknowledge your remarkable career in the military and your honorable service for all Americans. Being aware of what makes you a valuable employee makes all the difference in the world as you begin to plan your future.

Step 4: Talk to Your Chain of Command about Life after the Military

Now that you have taken the time to talk with your family and also started to look into what it will take to transfer your skills post-military, it is time to start talking to your current leaders to see what insights they can give you. You may be pleasantly surprised by how helpful they can be. Everyone you know knows someone else, and that person could be the one to help you or may know someone who can.

The main point is that you know someone right now who can have a positive impact on your discharge and job placement after the military.

> **Do not be afraid to talk to those around you about your plans after your ETS.**

I know you may think you are not viewed positively if you have decided not to reenlist or you have decided to retire, but deep down, your leaders should want you to succeed, even if it may not be under their watch.

Many veterans may also be afraid that they are leaving their friends behind, so leaving the military can be a very emotional decision. This is especially true for those who have been injured and may be receiving a medical discharge. The fact of the matter is that you are not letting your brothers and sisters down. Be proud of what you have accomplished, and realize that it is okay to serve your time and move on. Guilt is a completely normal feeling, but at some point, everyone ends up leaving the military for one reason or another.

That leads us back to talking to both your direct leadership team and your indirect leadership team about ideas for how you can best prepare for your ETS. Your direct leaders are your company commanders and also your company non-commissioned officers; they have valuable information you can use to shape further your plan of action. Your indirect leadership resources are your battalion commanders and the senior leadership even further out in your division (to use an army chain-of-command example, but this concept is applicable to all service branches).

You may think you know everything and do not need anyone's help, but that is just your military pride speaking. It is time you realize we all need someone in order to get from Point A to Point B. You cannot do it alone, and the sooner you realize that, the sooner you can get help from all the current direct influencers in your life.

We all need help at some point, so recognizing that you are entering a new phase of your life where you need others is extremely important. Your rank or service period does not matter; everyone around you can help. You could be an O5 and still be influenced by an E5. Once you have spoken with many members of your chain of command, you will start to realize how easy it can be to network internally to change your external results.

Step 5: Set Up an Appointment with a Career Adviser on Base

After talking things over with your chain of command to find out what resources are available to you, it is a great idea to start working with your career adviser on base. You should start working with your adviser anywhere from one year before your ETS date to a minimum of six months out. This time will give you the opportunity to start developing a solid resume and building a relationship with someone who can have a major impact on your future success. In fact, this connection may be one of the most important relationships for you to develop before you are discharged from the military.

Creating a resume, cover letter, and thank-you note for interviews to look professional will take you some time. They are not items you can just slap together. You have to edit, edit, and edit some more. You want your resume to shine when it is time to start submitting applications and resumes. You want your resume to stand out and for your experiences to be written in the civilian-sector language that most employers understand better than military jargon.

Most employers will not understand how your military experiences match the civilian job you are applying for, especially when you are compared to another applicant who has all civilian experiences. For this reason, you have to prepare well ahead of time so you can make your resume stand out. A base career adviser should be able to help you with this. A career adviser can help you not only with transferring your military skills but also with how to become qualified for a particular job you may be interested in. The adviser's job is to help you prepare for when you exit the military, so you should hold the adviser accountable to do so. Failure is not an option, and the squeaky wheel gets the grease.

You cannot and must not take no for an answer.

You were a valuable member of the military, and now you are about to be a valuable asset to an employer. You have to want the job more than the next man or woman with whom you are competing, and you must utilize all the resources available so you can show that to prospective employers both effectively and efficiently.

The last skill you must work on with a career adviser is your interviewing skills. You may have the best resume, but without perfecting what you will say and how you will say it during an interview, you could be passed over for a job you are qualified for.

As you can see, preparing for your future career is a process, and it is a very important process when you prepare to discharge. The time you put in now will pay off once you leave the comfort zone you had inside the military, where everything was set up for you the majority of the time.

Step 6: Contact a State Veteran Career Adviser Where You Will Be Relocating

The next person you want to contact as you continue to gather information is your state veteran representative in the vicinity of the city where you will be relocating. If you are staying in the same city where you currently are serving or if you are going back to your home of record, hopefully you already have an established relationship with this individual. The goal with all these connections is to create a network of people who will be instrumental to you in reaching your employment and ETS goals.

State veteran representatives are located in every state, and with the new hiring initiatives for veterans from the federal government, they should be very interested in helping you achieve success. It is their job to help you find the job that fits your qualifications. They should have established partnerships with both public and private sector employers all over your state. Their connections and resources are at your disposable as a veteran, and they can make all the difference when you need an inside advantage for a job announcement that is not publicized.

When you contact your state veteran representative, you want to find out the following information:

- What are the unemployment numbers for both veterans and non-veterans?
- What established relationships does the representative currently have in your field?
- What has been his or her success rate in placing veterans in your specific area?
- What specific state programs or resources are available that you can utilize?

This information is critical so you will be prepared when you settle back into the civilian workforce. Many veterans do not seek out this information until they have arrived where they plan to live, and then it takes them months to get oriented. You can start that process now, so when you get there, you will have the job lined up already.

You are really moving in the right direction now! Some veterans take years to recover from not taking some of the steps listed thus far.

When you are a young adult leaving the military with no direction, it seem an uphill battle, but it does not have to be. Regardless of your age or rank, the information provided will make a difference; finding out how it can help you specifically is key.

Step 7: Research and Collect Market Data for the Field You Will Be Entering

The last step in this chapter requires you to put forth the greatest amount of effort and energy. This step involves you doing the hard work to determine the most strategic way to attack your field. It is like owning your own business and having to collect the market analysis to determine what is the best way to reach your target market. You are doing the exact same thing here. You are utilizing all the information you have gained thus far so you can narrow down a list of possible jobs to the exact jobs you want to apply for.

This narrowing down can be a very lengthy process, but once achieved, it will give you a high level of satisfaction. Before you begin collecting data, talk with the career advisers on base to get access to all the latest databases you can use to gather all the information you will need in the quickest manner possible. Yes, you have hundreds of online search engine results to filter through. However, if you can streamline the process to get the quickest and most useful information, you should go that route.

Some of the resources available at the time of this printing are:

- Department of Veterans Affairs National Center for Veterans Analysis and Statistics: http://www.va.gov/vetdata/
- O*Net: https://www.onetonline.org
- USA Jobs: https://www.usajobs.gov
- Department of Labor Veterans' Employment and Training Service: http://www.dol.gov/vets/

These are some great resources and places to go to begin your search, but there are many more that can help you determine your best course of action moving forward. Please consult the resources section in the back of the book for more information. When you start early enough in the process, you definitely have an advantage over soldiers from all branches who decide to wait to find out this information.

★ ★ ★

You have learned many detailed steps on how to prepare yourself as a soldier transitioning into being a veteran in the civilian sector. It can be an uneasy period of your life, but if you follow some of the steps listed in this chapter, you will be ahead of the curve on many levels.

Staying positive and doing the little things will allow you to obtain the level of professional growth you desire and are attempting to reach by reading this book.

You may determine that you need more education as a result of your research, and that is okay. The key is to realize what you need to do so you can do it and have the success you want moving forward.

Chapter 2
Getting All Your
Personal Affairs in Order

*When I left the military and discharged from
active duty, I trusted that others would take the
right actions on my behalf. That was a mistake
because it took over a year to get my records
updated. I had failed to understand the importance of being properly prepared. I learned the
hard way, and looking back, knowing what I do
now, I would have done things differently.*

You have a very important job to do now that you have
committed to discharging from the military voluntarily
or involuntarily as the result of a traumatic injury. When you
first realize you are near the end of your enlistment, it can
be overwhelming and bring about a variety of different feelings and emotions. These next few months are going to set
the stage for you as you start to accept that the next chapter in
your life is about to begin.

Many of the steps in this chapter may seem obvious, but
you would be surprised by how many veterans have had a bad
experience with one or many of the steps necessary to leave
the military. You have to micromanage different elements of
your transition and allow yourself to be aware of everything
that is happening very quickly. One day, you are waking up for

another day in uniform, and the next, you are not. It happens that quickly.

Taking care of the little things will pay big dividends for you once you actually are out of the military.

Failing to take care of these steps could cause you major headaches, even up to a year after leaving. It is that serious. Not having the point of contact established with the departments that clear your paperwork and ultimately handle the main elements of your clearing process can be a huge mistake.

You need to have the contact information about the department and not just an individual. The person doing a certain job one day could be someone totally different a week from now, and this realization will not happen in most cases until after the fact. Imagine trying to track down your military records when every person whom you knew did that job in another place is gone. The new person has no idea who you are or what you are talking about. Yes, the new person will try to help you, but it will be a nightmare, regardless, in most cases. Follow these steps closely and you will thank yourself later.

7 Steps for Getting Your Personal Affairs in Order

1. Prepare yourself emotionally and physically.
2. Get all financial obligations settled.
3. Consolidate all your training and certification records.
4. Ensure all your awards and medals are documented.
5. Secure adequate living arrangements.
6. Take care of all shipping requirements for personal property.
7. Set up all travel arrangements.

Step 1: Prepare Yourself Emotionally and Physically

The hardest part about leaving the military is the psychological and physical aspect because your body may forever be changed as a result of your military service. It is best to accept this fact upfront instead of waiting to understand that your life will never be the same again. Is it a bad thing that it will never be the same? Not always, especially if you are able to take your experiences and make changes to your life for the better.

Having a strong will can sometimes prevent you from having the peace of mind you need to get through this transition. It is good to be determined, but not to the point of resisting the inevitable. You have to be willing to accept change and to deal with it in a positive way. To do this, you need to understand your limits and what you are willing to accept in exchange for your level of happiness moving forward.

Only you can balance the pros and cons of each decision that you make in determining what to change and what not to change. Thus, you should take the time to think about all the consequences, good and bad, before determining what your course of action should actually be.

The key is to think rationally to protect yourself and your family.

You may even need to talk to a professional to help you deal with this difficult period of your life, and that is okay. Sometimes, we all need to talk to someone to ensure we are emotionally stable.

It takes being prepared and having a healthy outlook on this transition to understand how your life will be different outside the daily regimen of military life you were used to, not only mentally but also physically. You have to ensure that you are eating properly and taking care of your body as well. Some injuries you may have endured may still be a part of your everyday life, and that could limit some of the activities you used to be able to do.

Looking at the bright side of things may seem daunting at this moment, but there is always a silver lining in life. You may have to dig deep to find out what that is for you. Your new life is just beginning, and once you can see through the smokescreen you must navigate to get to the other side, you will be okay. It may take some time to get all your thoughts together, but once you do, you will be stronger both emotionally and physically. Be strong and look forward to your future after the military. You can do it. You are not alone. You have hundreds, if not thousands, of your fellow veterans waiting back home who want to help you as well.

Step 2: Get All Financial Obligations Settled

One of the biggest aspects of any move from one city to another or from one job into another is the financial aspect of it all. Getting all your financial obligations settled is very important and necessary once you reach your ETS and leave the military. Hopefully, you had an opportunity to save/invest while you were serving or deployed. That would be the best-case scenario for any soldier.

The reality is that not every soldier has the ability or opportunities to do this during enlistment. With childcare expenses, unexpected vehicle costs, transportation costs for family members and themselves, and day-to-day living expenses, some soldiers end up being forced to live paycheck to paycheck, sometimes even while on deployment. This situation can be very difficult and especially take a toll on you emotionally and physically when you may be dealing with stress or depression from other issues on top of your finances.

You should start planning for your retirement or end of service enlistment at least a year out from your actual date of release. Even if you are only able to put away twenty dollars per paycheck, that is better than not doing anything at all. Being aware of your finances and where money is being spent is an area to look at during this transition period. You might be astonished by how much money you could be saving if you just cut back on the little things you may not really need.

As you draw closer to your ETS date, make sure all your final arrangements have been made, and pay all the bills from the city you are leaving to protect your credit. Although some bills may not yet be due and you may need to give a forwarding address, tie up all the loose ends you can before you transition to a new home. Protecting your credit is very important, and it has other ramifications outside credit worthiness.

For example, most employers look at credit reports to determine your overall value. Having a low credit score can actually hurt your ability to land a job that you may really want.

Therefore, it is extremely important to get all your financial obligations in order before it is too late.

Your move will be expensive enough, and if you do not have the cash on hand to afford the transition, you may have to use a few credit cards to help get you through. However, if you have to do that, be sure to have a repayment plan of action in place so you know how you will repay the money used. Credit cards or loans can be helpful if you have a plan. Remember the old saying, "Where there is a will, there is a way."

Step 3: Consolidate All Your Training and Certification Records

This next step is very important to your future success because what you learned during your military career needs to be documented. Without these records, you may have a hard time validating your skills, area of expertise, and qualifications once in the civilian sector. That is why you need to gather all your training records and all the certifications you received in the military prior to being discharged.

As stated previously, once you leave the military, it is very difficult to track down any information that is time sensitive in nature. Records for the most part are in paper format and have no physical trace outside the original copy. Recently, there has been a push to have all records digitally uploaded, but machines or computers can fail, as you know.

> **Nothing replaces the original hard copy that you should always have in your possession.**

To accomplish collecting all your records, it is very helpful to have had your records given to you at each step along the way while you served, most likely, in various duty stations around the world. Nothing is like getting that record at that exact moment in time versus years after the fact while trying to track down a record from another installation. More likely than not, an old record will be extremely difficult to duplicate after the fact unless it was recorded in a database that can be easily obtained by someone with access to the system.

While attempting to gather all your data, you should be aware of the importance of presenting all your records, prior to your ETS date, to ensure that your DD214 is properly updated with all your training records, awards, and certifications once generated by your branch of service prior to your ETS. The documentation you present will give you the opportunity to verify and correct the record before it is too late, because once you leave the military, your DD214 cannot be altered without submitting the documentation to the National Archives.

The process of updating your records after the fact requires you to file paperwork with the military service record National Archives (https://www.archives.gov/veterans/) with all the proof attached. This can take months to finalize, and the end result, if the evidence is there to support your request, will be a DD215 being issued to you. This result can be very cumbersome because now you have to keep track of your DD214 and DD215 to present to anyone who wants to verify your military status or certifications.

Another downside to updating your record after your ETS is that if a record is missing, you will also have to wait before you can list it on a resume, unless the person will accept the hard copy if you have it in your possession. If a record is not in your possession prior to leaving the military, you most likely will never have another chance to have that certification or record updated. So stay on top of this situation, because it will make a difference in your career post-military.

Step 4: Ensure All Your Awards and Medals Are Documented

Once you have ensured that all your training records are accounted for and you have the documentation to support the training you received in the military, it is time to focus on getting all your accomplishments squared away. Being able to account for your entire distinguished career of awards is very important. You do not want to miss out on any opportunities in the future to list your meritorious service medals on an application or resume.

The hardest part of being awarded a medal is having the paperwork included with the medal. Anyone can say that he did this or she did that in the military, but without the paperwork, you are going to have a hard time proving what you actually were recognized for. That is why gathering award letters is extremely important prior to your ETS date.

The paperwork is especially necessary from campaigns you served in. If your unit was part of a campaign in which everyone received an award, you still need to get that documentation. For example, if you served in Iraq or Afghanistan, you were part of a campaign that you can add to your award list. Going to your leaders is the first step, and a priority, to ensure you have the actual record associated with the campaign.

As with your military record for training, once you leave the military, it is extremely difficult to get your records updated without the proper documentation. Taking the time to account for these records before your ETS will allow you to move forward with confidence that your service record is complete. Some may say that awards mean nothing, but at the end of the day, you served America proudly and should be recognized for your efforts.

No one can take anything away from you one way or another, but you also never want to be called out for claiming a medal on your resume that you cannot prove you actually received. Paying attention to detail, as you know, makes all the difference in the world. Having a plan of action and setting up your affairs in a way that brings your amazing accomplishments to the forefront will only have positive impacts on your life moving forward.

You should be proud of the soldier you were; your awards are only half of the story but a very impactful piece of your career while you served.

Thank you for your service! It was and is not easy, nor can everyone make the sacrifices you have. You are a hero through and through, no matter the branch or length of your service to all Americans.

Step 5: Secure Adequate Living Arrangements

A big step in leaving the service is having your future residence lined up ahead of time. If you wait until the last minute or you are not prepared, you could run into some serious problems before you know it. Being able to have a home to call your own is a critical aspect as you plan your future. Whether that is in an apartment, renting a room temporarily, moving back in with a family member, or buying a home, you have to have a vision.

The four basic needs of life are food, water, air, and shelter. Having the ability to provide for yourself or you and your family is very necessary once you are discharged—whether honorably, medically, retiring, or dishonorably—from your service contract. You must find a way to meet these four needs and to do it in a relatively short period of time. You would be surprised how fast reality sets in once you leave the military. You will be in survival mode unless you are prepared ahead of time.

One important factor after deciding where you will relocate to is having a real sense of what part of the town you will be living in and how much you can afford per month for rent or a mortgage. If your income is going to be low and you will have to stay with a friend, it is a good thing to start having those conversations early to ensure you have a place to move to.

You should also have a backup plan for yourself in case something should fall through.

If you have had a significant or life-altering injury that may require modifications to a home or apartment, you should work with the VA hospital and organizations such as Wounded Warriors to get help with the equipment you may need so you can try to resume a normal life outside your injuries. Being a disabled veteran is not easy, but with the right attitude and the right amount of help from people who will be there for you no matter what, you can overcome any obstacle.

Having money saved to live comfortably is a good thing, but keep in mind that you should move somewhere reasonably affordable at first until you get everything situated and lined up as securely as possible for yourself and your family. Living expenses can pile up quickly, and job security is not what it used to be where employees stayed with companies for thirty-plus years. The job market is constantly changing, and that will also have an impact on what you can afford. Having a plan and continuing to work toward your goals sooner rather than later will allow you to have a successful transition.

Step 6: Take Care of All Shipping Requirements for Personal Property

Once you have secured a place to relocate to, you have to start thinking about getting your personal belongings organized to fill up your new home. The military usually takes care of all shipping costs, but you have to take the time to account for all your possessions. Veterans have told stories of valuable articles being lost during the shipment of their goods. Vehicles being shipped from an overseas duty station can be damaged as well.

So how do you help yourself out during this process? The first thing to do is consolidate all the receipts for all items over one hundred dollars and for all electronic devices you plan to ship. These expensive articles happen to be the items most commonly "missing" during the shipment of your goods. The second thing to do is inventory both on an electronic device and on paper for your records everything you own. That way when the shipper inventories your goods, you can cross-reference your list to ensure everything is documented correctly.

Finally, you want to take pictures of everything to prove that you actually owned the article and it was in good shape. You should also take pictures of the inside and outside of your vehicle if that is being shipped.

Save your pictures as proof in case any dispute arises about the condition of your car and/or goods once you receive them.

The last thing you want to have happen is not to receive the financial settlement, at the very least, when your personal items are gone forever. It is extremely difficult to accept when something is broken or missing, and some items that have sentimental value can never be replaced. You should try to take the most important items with you during your transition, such as laptops, electronic devices, and pictures you do not have backed up somewhere accessible.

Once your items are received at your new home, you need to go over every item and note exactly what you find. These steps will save you the aggravation and grief of not being prepared or of not knowing what could happen upon leaving the service. If you have to place your belongings in storage, you also need to inventory everything beforehand. Timelines exist for filing a claim, so be aware of them, along with how long the shipment of your goods will take.

Step 7: Set Up All Travel Arrangements
Once you reach this point, you are very close to starting a new chapter in your life, and that is not a bad thing if you are prepared. This brings us to the last step to consider prior to your ETS date—the task of booking all your travel arrangements through your travel agency for your specific branch. If you are staying in the town that your last duty station was in, your travel arrangements might not be very elaborate outside of driving a few miles to get to your accommodations.

★ ★ ★

Many thoughts will likely be running through your mind at this point, and you may even be reconsidering a few or most of the decisions you have made that have led you to the end of your service. You may be having some of the following thoughts:

- Should I have reenlisted?
- Will I be able to find the job I want upon my discharge?
- Am I doing the right thing by leaving my friends to serve without me?

All those thoughts are valid and real. There is no shame in having these thoughts, and to be honest, leaving the military is not an easy decision. Many veterans look back with regret when they have to leave the military for medical reasons or when they decide to leave early and later wish they didn't. You always have the option to get back in the service with your original branch or another branch if you choose in the future, but there may be some consequences, such as the loss of a Veterans Affairs medical disability rating or a loss of rank as a result.

You also have to remember that no guarantee exists that you will be accepted back into the military. So if you are not 100 percent sure you are ready for an ETS, maybe you should talk to your friends and family about your decision before it is too late. You do not want to rush into any drastic decisions, but you do want to ensure that all possibilities have been explored. Even if you choose to stay in the military after going through all the steps we have discussed, that may not be a bad decision if that is what you really want. Ultimately, only you know what is right for you and your family.

If you choose to stick with your initial or gut feeling about moving on, realize that you are about to venture into a world that is different from the one you may have known when you left. As you know, change is inevitable, and only time will tell what is right or wrong moving forward.

The key is to make the most out of your decision and to maximize all the opportunities for your life moving forward.

The moment you step on that plane or train or start your car after clearing your post and turning in your weapon, it will finally hit you that you are going from soldier to veteran in that exact moment. The future is yours for the taking! With a concise action plan, you will have a fulfilled life full of success. Stay vigilant and be prepared every step of the way.

Chapter 3
Medical Documentation Preparation

I had no idea about the importance of documenting everything that occurred to me physically and psychologically during my enlistment. It took me almost a year to realize that my life would never be the same because of the physical limitations I had from numerous injuries and constant wear and tear on my "army strong" body as a mechanized infantry soldier.

As you begin this leg of your journey, be aware and stay prepared for what lies ahead for you. The information contained in this chapter will make a difference in your life moving forward after the military. You do not want to be that veteran who is having problems and ends up fighting the Veterans Affairs Administration for upwards of five-plus years, going through the lengthy backlog appeal process, all because you do not have the proper medical documentation.

The information and data you will be collecting is vital to you and your family moving forward. Please take all the necessary steps outlined in this chapter to help ensure you have the best information available if you need to file a disability claim as a result of an accident you endured during your service to America. You will have veterans who have your back all day, and they will help you fight the new war that could be a reality for you once you get back home.

Filing a disability claim or receiving any proper medical care is a process, and having representation and support from your fellow veterans is very important. That is why having a veteran organization representing you, such as the Disabled American Veterans or the American Legion, to name a couple, is very important. These organizations really will fight on your behalf and go the extra mile to help you once you take the initiative to contact them for assistance. Therefore, do not be scared of the process, but rather, get prepared by helping yourself and trusting that these military veteran affiliates will be there as trusted friends to help you.

It takes a team effort and concentrated approach to get the benefits you deserve.

Sometimes, because the Veterans Affairs claims processing system is so weighed down with thousands of disability claims, being compensated properly even for an outward disability can be a battle. It is a crazy process and one that is not perfect by any means. I think the Veterans Affairs means well in most cases, but you never know whether the final decision will classify you as a veteran with a disability or conclude that you are not.

That is why you have to keep standing up for what you believe to be true, no matter what the initial outcome, because you always have the option to appeal any decision rendered on your behalf. It does not have to be difficult if you have the information to support your claim, and when you are proactive, it should be a much easier process than trying to recreate the wheel after the fact. Always remember that there is no shame in reporting an illness or medical problem as a soldier or civilian, post-military service. Your life

is valuable, and everyone who served has a right to be compensated for his or her sacrifices.

7 Steps for Collecting Your Medical Records

1. Gather all previous medical records and field
   reports from accidents you were in.
2. Research the specific injuries and/or symptoms you have.
3. Prepare for your final physical examination.
4. Take your final physical examination.
5. Get a second opinion if you feel the doctor did
   not properly diagnose your disability and/or
   symptoms.
6. Follow up with your doctor to clarify your
   findings.
7. Finish collecting complete documentation from
   any exams or tests you had prior to your ETS.

Step 1: Gather All Previous Medical Records and Field Reports from Accidents You Were In

At the very moment you are life-flighted out of a battle
zone or receive treatment in the field for an injury, the next
chapter of your life has just begun, whether you know it
or not. The steps you take after these intense moments are
critical to your life outside the military and the future you
will have with your family. It is not easy with most traumatic injuries, physical injuries, or psychological wounds
from war for a person to recover or heal and find peace.
However, the truth is you can heal and find peace in your
own unique way with time and a strong faith in your purpose in this world.

The key is finding a balance between healing and having peace in your heart. This process begins when you can gather all the proof of what you have endured that only you know and understand through your medical records history report. Your medical records tell a story of not only what you have battled throughout your life in the military but also your resiliency to overcome adversity. You are stronger today than you were yesterday, and tomorrow you will be even stronger.

As soon as you are healthy enough to think clearly, you need to start gathering the facts of what you just went through. It will be like solving a mystery because you will not have all the facts. That is why you must start right away to connect the dots to find out exactly what has happened to you mentally and physically. Memories and stories fade, but medical records tell the story and connect the dots clearly if captured correctly, based on firsthand accounts or actual medical records for any procedures you underwent. Secondhand information will not be helpful in making future claims; thus witness statements with firsthand recollection of what occurred are best in corroborating the details of an incident. After you have solved the puzzle, you immediately need to start gathering all your documentation and medical records. In addition, you need to capture every record along your road to recovery at every appointment or soon after. Since most recordkeeping is becoming electronic, that should make it even easier to capture records without delay.

If your ETS date is near and you have not kept up with your records, it is time to go over every injury you endured and try to piece together the story after the fact. If your records were maintained correctly, you may be in luck, and everything may be available upon request. If not, you have a lot of work ahead of you.

Do not grow tired—every record you uncover or gain access to is like a piece of gold you were able to find. Please do not just say, "Whatever. Who cares anyway?"

You have an entire military community who cares about you and your quality of life moving forward.

Your life is very meaningful; and giving up before you face the real challenges ahead is not an alternative. You have options, so use every resource you have to gather and maintain these critical clues involving the pain or injuries you received as a member of the United States Military.

Step 2: Research the Specific Injuries and/or Symptoms You Have

After you have gathered your entire military medical records, it is time to move on to phase two of your transition from military to civilian life. You are at a very good place, but you are not out of the woods yet. The reason is that, before you can go forth from the military, you have to prepare for your last physical within your specific branch of service. This exam is critical for evaluating the exact symptoms you are dealing with.

That is why you need to be knowledgeable about your symptoms and be prepared for what the exam will encompass. You can make a blanket statement such as "I have a traumatic brain injury from an IED (improvised explosive device)," or you could make the following statement, "I had a traumatic brain injury in 2005 from an IED explosion, and my symptoms are depression, anxiety, difficulty sleeping, sweaty palms, nightmares, headaches, sensitivity to light and sound, difficulty making friends, and thoughts of suicide." These are two very different statements. The latter explains exactly what you are dealing with, and all that needs to be documented completely.

Do not be afraid of what others may think or how you will be perceived!

You are a proud United States soldier, and your health is a priority that every citizen of America must accept.

Your health concerns and problems are real, so they need to be addressed immediately. The quicker they are addressed, the quicker you can be rehabilitated in an effective manner with a treatment plan in place that is meant to help you, not destroy you.

Not one veteran should look down on himself or herself because of physical or mental limitations based on service to our country. Rather, all veterans should feel a sense of pride in doing their very best, no matter the obstacle they encountered. In addition, veterans need to realize that reaching out for help is not a sign of weakness but, rather, a sign of strength that comes from knowing the struggles we face today shape our happiness and future tomorrow.

So prior to you having your physical, you need to research exactly what you are dealing with on a daily basis. Doing this important step will go a long way toward your recovery if you were injured or scarred for life in any way. When you go into the physical, you can be open and honest, and hopefully, you will view it as a discovery process in which you learn very important information about your diagnosis. You are not a doctor, but you can find out important information that could be vital for your future treatment once you have left the military.

Step 3: Prepare for Your Final Physical Examination

Preparing for your physical examination should not be taken lightly, as if it is another "check the box" event toward clearing yourself to be discharged. In the past, most soldiers were probably not aware of the ramifications of not taking things seriously for this part of the ETS process. How could you know, as a discharging service member, what your physical examination would mean for you once you leave the military unless someone tells you?

What it means is that if you have any serious medical conditions, or even minor ones, for that matter, they need to be documented and addressed in your physical exam.

It is critical that every inch of your body is given a complete and thorough examination.

If you miss your opportunity to have your injuries and/ or symptoms diagnosed, then once discharged, you may never have another opportunity to plead your case, and that will make it extremely difficult to receive proper service or treatment connected to a disability that occurred during your military service.

Many veterans—from World War II veterans to more recent Iraq and Afghanistan veterans—would have paid good money to have this information available to them. The War on Terror did not occur solely on the battlefield; for those soldiers who were deployed to those regions, it still lives in their minds and bodies. It is very difficult to have the fortitude to say, as a "proud, lean, mean fighting machine," that you may have anxiety, depression, or PTSD.

Those are the symptoms of a soldier who has been torn down, built back up, and then lived through some very traumatic events throughout a distinguished military career. You have nothing to be ashamed of. Being open and honest during your final physical examination is very important. How can a medical professional post-military know what is wrong if a soldier's problem was not addressed during his or her service career? Doctors can only assume it is not military-related if it is not documented correctly during this phase of your ETS.

One last thing to remember is that most scars are internal, but the pain you feel is only known through external communications. You must take the time to verbalize exactly what you are feeling and where. You only have one body and one mind. The feelings, pain, and emotions that your body is dealing with have to be identified or addressed through medical evaluations. It may be hard to attend appointment after appointment and get the runaround about what you are dealing with. It may take an enormous amount of your time to get a proper diagnosis; in some cases, the doctors may never be able to pinpoint the cause of your problems. However, please do not give up on your body or mind. You are a valuable person in this world, so you deserve to be cared for by the country you served. No soldier deserves to be brushed over or treated like a number on a piece of paper, so taking this step seriously is key.

Step 4: Take Your Final Physical Examination
Now that you have properly prepared yourself psychologically, emotionally, and physically, it is time to have your final ETS physical exam. If you have prepared adequately, you should be able to communicate exactly and precisely what your symptoms and/or conditions are. If you are not prepared, you are at a disadvantage, but it is not too late yet.

Your actual exam is your opportunity to put everything you have endured during your military service on record. This is your chance to identify and explain what you are facing on a daily basis that may not yet have been included in your medical records, or worse, may have been lost in the fog of war during your enlistment.

Your physical examination is the best chance you have to be substantiated, once you go through the Veterans Administration claims and benefits process, post-ETS, to prove the validity of your medical claim for service disability.

To prove your case so you can receive medical services, the US Department of Veterans Affairs will look at all your military medical service records, which in most cases are electronic now, to determine whether a basis exists for confirming your claim. Your ETS physical examination will be included in those medical records, which will make it easier for you to receive the services you need after your service; therefore, it is imperative that you have everything documented. This is your chance to have your side of the story heard before it is too late. It is also your chance to have the evidence documented to support your claim of what exactly your medical ailments are.

During your examination, do not allow yourself to be intimidated or made to feel that what you have to say is unimportant. What you have endured is important, and it needs to be heard LC ("loud and clear" in military terms). If the doctor conducting your exam is not properly qualified to diagnosis or capture what you are dealing with, ask to see a specialist to have that information included, or ask for a second opinion from another doctor if the first is trying to ignore your feedback on your medical condition.

Having this information on the record will make your life that much easier once you leave the military. The backlog for veterans who are battling and fighting to have their benefits awarded is in the thousands. What you are doing now will pay off for you down the road, and the claims process will be that much easier because of your action during this critical phase of preparing for your ETS. Having your medical records in order is only one aspect of attending to your health welfare, but it will give you a distinct advantage over other veterans who have not done so and wish they had before they left the service.

Step 5: Get a Second Opinion If You Feel the Doctor Did Not Properly Diagnose Your Disability and/or Symptoms

Sometimes, the doctor you see for your exam may not be the best advocate for your situation. Under these circumstances, it is time for you to be proactive and face the difficult task of standing up for what you believe to be right. If you do not feel comfortable with your physical examination and its results, you should voice your concern to the doctor during the exam or immediately after. This is your battle to overcome in a strategic and productive manner to reach your end result, which is to have your injuries documented correctly.

Hopefully, once you voice your concerns with the first doctor, follow-up appointments will be scheduled, or you can request to have a different doctor make an evaluation on your medical injuries and conditions that you are dealing with. Most times, scheduling such appointments is not even an issue, but you should be prepared in case it is. Too much information is never a bad thing in this situation.

The key is to be ready for what could come without becoming anxious as you know the how the system can work both for you and against you in some instances.

Preparing the medical elements for your ETS can be very stressful, but having information on your side to help you navigate through these murky waters is like having a lifejacket in the middle of the ocean. At least you have a fighting chance once you are aware of what you are up against.

So what should be your course of action if the doctor you see for your exam is uncooperative in your quest to document all your service-connected injuries prior to your ETS? The following steps are on an as-needed basis.

First, go to your direct supervisor and explain the situation. He or she may or may not be sympathetic to your problem, but who cares? You are about to leave the military anyway. Let nothing stop you, within reason and your legal limits, from getting proper evaluations of your injuries. This is important documentation that you will have in your file for the rest of your life.

Hopefully, your supervisor will do the right thing and get you connected with the people who need to make the decisions in regard to your claim. You could always break rank and use your high chain of command's open door policy to go directly to the commanding officer about your concerns and present your case in a professional manner. The goal is to get the problem solved with the least amount of resistance as possible. Nine times out of ten, this approach will work, and you will have the second opinion you want. The goal is to have your voice heard and make sure the real issues are addressed in regard to your health.

One thing to remember is that one physician's determinations can be reversed by another doctor's decision. Therefore, if you do not agree with the medical findings of the first or second opinion, you always have the option to go to another doctor, outside the military at your own cost most likely, for a third opinion to get his or her medical interpretation as well. This can be done, preferably, before you leave the military, but you could also do this post-ETS through either the VA hospital if you are being seen there for your medical treatments or your private primary care physician's office in your home of record.

Step 6: Follow Up with Your Doctor to Clarify Your Findings

Once you have the opinion you feel most comfortable with, make sure you understand everything in the reports about your physical examinations. That could end up being extensive, depending on how many appointments you went through. If you have any questions about them, such as the terminology used by the physician, then arrange a follow-up visit to the doctor to clarify everything. It is important to understand how the military perceives your injuries in light of the symptoms you are experiencing from any traumatic events that occurred during your years of service.

What you do now is critical for your psychological and physical well-being, post-military. The actions you take at this point center on having a medical opinion you trust.

> **Truly grasping your condition and how you can recover and heal without 100 percent dependency on medication, if possible, depending on the severity of your injuries, can go a long way towards improving your life as you effectively manage your pain, injuries, and condition.**

It might not be easy to take care of all these doctors' appointments, but after your service to our country, it is your entitlement. The government is obligated to get your records in order prior to your discharge. If that does not happen—and it has not happened in the past for too many veterans who did not have the knowledge at their fingertips—it is an epic failure you cannot afford.

Be prepared for the upcoming follow-up appointment once it is scheduled. Take the time to research exactly what was determined and how the physician came to his or her overall conclusions based on your initial evaluations. Go prepared to ask questions and have a candid dialogue with the physician about your symptoms and/or condition in more detail. The more information you know, the better off you will be for a treatment plan once you are back home and released from active or reserve duty.

You always have the option to get an organization such as the American Legion or the Disabled American Veterans to represent you in the case of any discrepancies between the findings of the physician during your out-processing and any other doctor visits or medical opinions you have gathered.

> **The key thing to remember is that the sooner you make a decision and move forward, the better chance you will have to prove your medical case with the US Department of Veterans Affairs down the line.**

You will be encouraged to know that many veterans and their family members have been there and done that, so they can point you in the right direction in terms of protecting your life, limbs, and health against any adversaries who do not have your best interest at heart.

Step 7: Finish Collecting Complete Documentation from Any Exams or Tests You Had Prior to Your ETS

Collecting your medical documentation has been such a journey thus far that you are probably ready just to be done and move forward into the next chapter of your life. However, your health and medical records collection is the most important information to have in place when you leave your career in the US Armed Forces.

You have made many sacrifices, so you should walk away knowing that you sacrificed your time, family, and health for a greater cause, and you should always be proud of that. That is why gathering and analyzing your records is so important. Do not let any stone go unturned in your quest to uncover all the facts regarding your health. These steps can go a long way in ensuring that you get the care you need and deserve once you return to the civilian world.

★ ★ ★

You should have collected all your records and gotten copies of all tests that were completed by this time. If so, then you are as prepared as you could ever be to leave the military with your head held high and your shoulders straight. Pause to reflect on what you enjoyed and what you will miss about your time in service. Remember that you cannot go back to the past, and now your life will never be the same. There is definitely a transition period, mentally and physically, once you are fully discharged. It is not easy to break away from such a regimented daily lifestyle. It will take some time to get used to, and aspects of that lifestyle will likely stay with you forever.

Blocking out any bad memories or experiences can be harder to do than even the mentally strongest person will admit.

Talking about your feelings and opening up to someone you trust can be extremely helpful in dealing with any emotional or physical pain.

Do not be afraid to talk about your feelings, whether you are a male or female veteran. Getting help is important if you are dealing with something you cannot solve alone, and in the long run, it should be very beneficial.

Phase 2
★ ★ ★

Personal and Professional Growth as a Civilian

Chapter 4
Psychological Well-Being

Over the years since my discharge from active duty, I have come to realize that the scars from my military career will never go away. It has forever been beaten into my body and mind that I will be a US soldier for the rest of my life. However, I have also come to realize that I can make life a lot easier on myself by not focusing on the negative aspects of daily dealing with my physical and emotional pain as a disabled veteran. I do this by focusing my thoughts on productive or positive aspects of my life, the best I can; that way I can make better decisions.

Your mind is a very complex and sophisticated machine that, like a car, needs to be well maintained for optimal performance. The military lifestyle took a toll on you, both physically and mentally. That is why it is extremely important to take care of your mental well-being, in addition to your body, moving forward, just as you do when you take your car to the garage for semi-annual maintenance.

Your psychological well-being is extremely important and should never be taken for granted. You need your mind for everything, so if you have a chemical imbalance in your thought processes or a breakdown in how you handle difficult situations, there could be significant repercussions. The good news is that there are ways to train your mind and people you can reach out to for help in improving your mental sharpness.

In the army, they tell you to be "army strong." This concept applies to many areas of a soldier's life: physically, emotionally, and psychologically. You are trained to "be all you can be" and to suck it up to drive on. That is all fine and dandy, but there are also mental consequences from the mindset instilled in every member of the US Armed Forces to never give up, keep fighting, and always suck it up in the face of adversity.

The problem is that your mind can take only so much "sucking it up." Everyone is trained to be a "lean, mean, fighting machine," which is great on paper, but there are drawbacks to this approach. The truth is that no one is or ever was a machine. Soldiers are human beings just like everyone else on Earth; they have pain, and they make mistakes. The bottom line is that everyone deals with adversity differently.

After you leave the military, you have to be aware of these facts and not be ashamed of any feelings or fears you may be dealing with. They are only natural.

You are not alone. Many other veterans are experiencing some of the same emotional and psychological pitfalls.

You never want to consider suicide as a way out. There are people and processes in place for veterans that can help you overcome any obstacle. Those outlets will be addressed in this chapter, so you can learn how a veteran in pain can get help and, in time, have a full recovery.

7 Steps Toward Mental Stability

1. Evaluate your situation upon leaving the military.

2. Talk to friends, family, or other military veterans who may be going through similar traumatic experiences about your feelings and any concerns you may have.

3. Talk to a doctor or clinical physician through the VA hospital or in outside private care who specializes in veteran care.

4. Attend veteran-based groups to observe how others are dealing with various types of post-military effects from service.

5. Develop strategies to cope and overcome obstacles.

6. Research the effects any medications may have on your mood or overall health, good or bad.

7. Set up an action plan for how you will get through this period of your life.

Step 1: Evaluate Your Situation upon Leaving the Military

The day has finally come, and you are free—which may be good or bad, depending on your viewpoint. You are no longer under contract with the United States of America. You are now going to be exposed to new life experiences and circumstances outside of what you have grown accustomed to. This process is one you will have to get used to.

Many soldiers struggle with this transition, so it is nothing to be ashamed of.

It is not easy to transition from a military environment to the reality of civilian life.

However, you can be in control of your transition and how you cope with this change. Having acquired a strong mental focus from the military is one asset you can use to your advantage. This same strength can also be a detriment to your mental health if used to keep you from facing some issues early on. Toughing it out may not be the best approach. The key aspect to remember is not to let pride get in the way of settling into your new life.

You may ask, "How do I do that?" Your mental toughness was contingent on many factors in the military, such as protection, security, safety, and survival. In the civilian world, you have the same factors to consider, minus the life-or-death aspect that usually goes along with being a soldier. Now, you have to evaluate each situation, be willing to let your toughness drop as you examine where you can use help, and then stay focused on getting the help you may need.

Only you know the consequences of events you experienced during your time of service. That is why understanding your limitations will go a long way toward determining your capacity to be mentally tough post-military. To understand what you are dealing with on a personal, family, or professional level, it is a good idea to write down some thoughts on paper initially so you can properly analyze what you are actually dealing with.

Now is the time—today, not tomorrow—to evaluate exactly how you need to proceed. Do you need to talk to someone about a problem you are having? Do you need to get more information about benefits, or do you just need to be around people who understand you? These are all valid questions that begin with you. Once you have your list accumulated, review your thoughts and be prepared to share what you have discovered with a close friend or relative to help you determine your next course of action.

Step 2: Talk to Friends, Family, or Other Military Veterans Who May Be Going Through Similar Traumatic Experiences about Your Feelings and Any Concerns You May Have

One of the best parts of being a veteran is that you do not have to look far to find someone who has served his or her country as well. This is great news as you look to grow and expand your network of friends once you return home. Veterans always seem to know how to handle the most difficult problems or how to get through adversity positively, which is why connecting with those who will understand you more than anyone is critical to mental stability.

You may have experienced certain things in the military that you will never want to talk about again. That is completely normal. However, holding your feelings, thoughts, or emotions in can take a toll on anyone who is dealing with a traumatic experience or life-changing event. A medical doctor or Veterans Affairs physician may have to be your first option for mental stability, but initially talking to others is usually also a great starting point.

You may think that your family and friends back home will never understand. That may be true, but for the most part, those support channels are a great way to release some of the pain that may have built up. Also, your family and friends really are your biggest supporters because they want you to be both healthy and happy. Trusting others is an important part of opening up to anyone, especially family. You may never want your loved ones to know about what you saw or heard in battle or in a hostile situation.

Even a simple action like pushing a button on a ship may have psychological effects based on what that action led to in terms of death or property destruction. Memories of such situations can be a huge burden to carry around. Your family or close friends may not need to know all the exact details, but they could be a good resource to release some of your fears and feelings to in a safe, controlled environment.

If you decide you will not talk to anyone close to you, the next step is to seek to confide in your military connections. This could happen back home with a group of veterans you join or with people you served with. The latter may be the best option because this band of brothers and sisters will have your back for the rest of your life.

It is not easy to deal with pain and mental anguish. If you get to the point where you feel you cannot talk to anyone, always remember this one thing:

You are never alone in this world! There is always someone somewhere who will be there for you. There is no mission too difficult and no sacrifice too great in terms of one veteran helping another veteran in need.

Step 3: Talk to a Doctor or Clinical Physician through the VA Hospital or in Outside Private Care Who Specializes in Veteran Care

After talking it over with your friends and loved ones, you may come to the conclusion that it is time to seek further medical or mental treatment to help you with your recovery process. In order to get care through the VA hospital, you must first register with it. You can do this online or by contacting the hospital directly. Most likely, an initial visit will then be scheduled for you to fill out paperwork and be registered in the system.

Once you are in the system, you will most likely be assigned a primary care provider to assess your needs before putting in the proper consultations you will need. If you are already registered, then you are ahead of the game, which is wonderful. If not, you will need to go through this lengthy process, which, unfortunately, can sometimes be cumbersome. One thing to remember is if you move or switch VA hospitals, you will have to be reregistered in the particular hospital where you are seeking care. The good news is that your medical records should be in an electronic format, which should make the transition easier.

At the time of this printing, the VA is under a lot of heat for failing to meet the needs of the veterans in the system. This situation has raised several questions about the wait times for veterans seeking timely health care. The goal should be to expedite the process so veterans can receive the care they need without having to go through a lengthy process. That being said, under the current process, after your visit with the health care provider, it should not be long before you are scheduled for the PTSD clinic or a visit with the appropriate medical doctor, psychologist, or psychiatrist.

If you choose to bypass all the red tape and see outside healthcare providers for your treatment, that may be the best decision, provided you have outside health insurance or you have the financial means to do so.

Either way, the main goal is to have an outlet to talk to someone regarding you emotional and mental well-being.

Knowing whom to trust and having options for dealing with the adversity you may be facing is extremely important to your recovery.

Building trust with the medical professional who is working with you, no matter the route you take, is important for overcoming barriers that may be holding you back from getting your true emotions and feelings out so you can heal. It is not easy to open up, especially to a complete stranger, about extreme circumstances you experienced. Healing is a process that takes time. The important thing to remember is that you can talk about as little or as much as you want during these visits. The primary focus should be on you and helping you to move forward with your life.

Step 4: Attend Veteran-Based Groups to Observe How Others Are Dealing with Various Types of Post-Military Effects from Service

Now that you have hopefully reached out to the appropriate medical professional to help you deal with any problem or difficulty you are having, it is time to consider other avenues. It is important to consider all possible options that could help you go down a road toward a full recovery. One option at your disposal is joining a veterans group that meets to discuss similar problems.

You can find specific information on websites such as the Department of Veterans Affairs PTSD: National Center for PTSD (http://www.ptsd.va.gov) for how to sign up for such a group. In addition, you can also get connected with a group directly through the VA hospital or your medical provider. The main point is that resources are available to help you so you are not dealing with anxiety, depression, feelings of guilt or being alone, etc.

> **Trying to overcome the fear of talking to others is understandable, but the benefits of doing so far outweigh not doing anything at all.**

As a veteran and soldier, as stated earlier, it is difficult to open up in a private setting, let alone a group setting. However, with time, it may become easier and easier to talk things over with people who are going through similar circumstances.

You could start by talking to other veterans or your friends about the idea of being enrolled in such a program. The positive aspect to remember is that if you try a group and do not like it or feel uncomfortable in it, you can wait to return when the situation is right for you. You could also consider a different group more in line with the problems you are dealing with, if the one you attended was not helpful.

The main thing to realize is that you can find positive avenues to help you cope with psychological and emotional pain during your transition period from military to civilian life. Talking through your fears is better than letting your feelings be pushed to the bottom. We are all strong veterans, but we also all have our breaking points that can be exposed when we become overwhelmed. Having options is a good thing, and with veteran support, you can get through this period of your life successfully.

Step 5: Develop Strategies to Cope and Overcome Obstacles
One of the best ways to deal with adversity and tragedy is through a process of discovering who you are and what you are really made of. Learning to cope and to deal with adversity is not easy, but just like in the military, if you break it down to the lowest level and simplify it, you can come up with a strategy or plan that is both efficient and effective. The same model can be applied in this situation with a slight variation in order to specify exactly what you are trying to accomplish: to have a clear mind that is not consumed by the events of the past.

Talking to people and meeting in a group setting can greatly benefit your healing phase as a veteran. Taking it to the next level is equally important. You may ask, "How do I get through the grief? How do I get out of bed every day?" These are valid questions, and the basic answer is, "You do it one day at a time." Eventually, it does get easier, and life does go on. All that really matters is that you take as long as you need to feel good again while receiving the help you need for your recovery.

Developing your strategies is basically like have building blocks that you organize in your personal life to maintain your sanity. This process may come easily for some, but for others, it may take time to accomplish such a mission of getting control of your life again. Having a plan for how to approach the day is the best way to deal with adversity, and when you master your ability to control your emotions, you know your plan is working.

Planning for your day beginning with when you wake up in the morning is important. Having a planner in your phone or on a written calendar can help you be organized and also keep your mind occupied so you don't let negative thoughts control you. Your mind controls your body and your actions.

When you keep your thoughts active and positive, you will see good results.

Looking at it from the other side, when you have negative thoughts and do not have activities to keep your mind off the pain or emotional stress you are facing, you can experience a great amount of stress, anxiety, and depression. Staying focused on your recovery and moving forward is a healthy way to regain control of your life. There is no shame in doing so, and you are not taking away from anyone or denying anything that occurred in the military. Your brothers and sisters in the armed forces will always be your battle buddies. Moving on is okay; in fact, when you do so, it has a positive impact by encouraging others to do so as well.

Step 6: Research the Effects Any Medications May Have on Your Mood or Overall Health, Good or Bad

You are learning a lot of information that can be extremely important in your recovery. Now it is time to address another significant aspect that can help you reach your goals: prescribed medication. While receiving medical care, you may be prescribed certain medications to help with pain, anxiety, depression, or other issues.

Medication may be a good solution for helping you cope, but you must first analyze the drugs to make sure they will not further complicate things for you now or in the future. This step is very important and cannot be ignored for any reason.

Your health is priority #1 so finding out every possible side effect of a medication should be important to both you and your family. Medication is not something to play with, and if not handled correctly, it can have drastic consequences.

Everyone's body and chemical makeup are different. That is why one drug that works for one person may not work for another. Medications usually have a laundry list of side effects that could lead to horrific issues that are a nightmare to endure. For that reason, researching the drug prescribed is extremely important, along with discussing it with both your doctor and pharmacist.

After researching the drug and talking about it, you can make the decision to move forward with a particular drug you believe can help you with the least amount of risk to your health. Experimenting with drugs is not good, but in some instances, it may be necessary to find the drug that works best with your symptoms through regulated doses prescribed by your doctor. The key is to find a mix of drugs and therapy that works best for you with the least amount of problems.

If you have to take medication, hopefully it will not be for a long time. If it is required over a long period, monitor your intake to ensure you experience positive results.

It is always a good idea to communicate constantly with your doctor or physician and notify him or her of any changes in your diet or health as a result of the medications you are taking.

This communication will help you keep the side effects to a minimum.

Step 7: Set Up an Action Plan for How You Will Get through This Period of Your Life

Everyone has a unique way of expressing himself or herself and mapping out a plan for how to overcome adversity. What is that method for you? Is it writing it down on a piece of paper? Is it thinking about it first and then talking over your ideas with someone close to you? Or is it simply through faith and putting 100 percent trust in believing that with God's help you can change your life? It may even be a combination of these methods and others not mentioned.

There is no set method that is better than another, but the key is having a plan that has worked in the past and discovering what will work for you in the future. When dealing with trauma and pain, though difficult, it does not have to mean the end of everything good around you. What makes you happy and what brings you joy in this world is yours. You are in control for the most part of only you, and understanding what makes you, *you* is very important as you begin to have a more positive outlook on your situation and life overall.

Many other veterans are facing similar challenges, so your ability to turn the corner may also impact another veteran in a positive manner. No matter what you are going through, planning is the one aspect that you can perfect for your absolute well-being to be restored as closely as possible to who you were before whatever caused you to be in the circumstances you are facing now. Life improvement is never easy, but it also can be very rewarding once you make the choice to be free again.

The pain and memories of what you experienced may never go away. However, every veteran deserves to live a life full of joy, peace, and love. You can achieve this by taking a simple three-step approach to healing:

1. Love yourself again.
You have to value and appreciate the great person you are. No one on Earth can take that away from you, and knowing the good you bring the world is vital to moving forward.

2. Separate the pain of what occurred and the reality of today.

You cannot change the past, but you can change the future. Your actions now will allow you, over time, to see the good in the world, despite the evil all around us.

3. The last step is taking strides every day to reach your goals, whatever they may be.

Create your very own Veterans Personal Guide for Survival Kit. In this kit, include all the items or components of your life that help you tackle every day. They may include the smile in your children's eyes, a good book to read on the couch or in bed to try to relax, or the embrace of a loved one. No matter what, never give up on yourself; you are 100 percent of value.

Discovering who you are and what exactly you are made of will be realized as you return to civilian life. Being positive and appreciating the good things will carry you further than you ever thought possible. Following the steps outlined in this chapter, along with having a well-thought-out action plan, will really help you get through the difficult moments you may be facing.

Knowing what *you* want and how you will get there is very important. Utilizing all the resources you have at your disposal is critical in coming to grips with physical and emotional pain. Life is extremely difficult, and adding on the stress from military life makes it that much harder. You are going to get through this because you are not alone.

Any veteran in need can find someone to talk to throughout his or her journey. Having a mentor or sponsor is also a great idea in order to have a direct connection with someone who is in your corner whenever you need him or her, regardless of the time of day. The decisions you make today will ultimately affect your tomorrow, which means that your plan needs to cover all points of contact in order to keep you moving forward.

★ ★ ★

Life throws us some weird curve balls, is not fair, and can also be very unforgiving sometimes. No matter the difficult circumstance in your life, an answer always exists that will make things better. Sometimes it takes time, but when you get through the storm, you can look back and realize how determined a person you are. Despite all you have endured, you are a valuable person in this world.

Your life has meaning, and you can never go back in time, but you can do better the next time. The pain you may be dealing with may seem as if it will never go away, but it will eventually. Therefore, do yourself a favor and do not dwell on the negativity, but focus on the positives that will help you move forward regardless of what is going on around you. Know that you are a strong veteran who served his or her country proudly despite extreme circumstances.

Chapter 5
Education and Certification via the GI Bill

It took me nine years of being out of the military before I overcame my fear of going back to college to get any type of degree. I really wish my educational benefits had been properly explained to me prior to my leaving the military. I had no idea how beneficial using my GI Bill and Post-9/11 GI Bill could be. I am so thankful that I went back to school and for the veteran who explained everything I had missed about how the program actually works to help all veterans post-military service. As a result of the knowledge I gained, I am passing on to you the same road map that led me to receiving a bachelor of science degree in business administration and a master's in human resources and employment relations.

One of the biggest keys to success in life is education. As the old saying goes, "Knowledge is power."

However, education is not easily obtained due to costs, time commitments, and life's distractions. Fortunately, your military service can play an important role in helping you to reach your future goals. Not only are you a proud veteran, but you also have the keys to your future in your hands with the GI Bill or Post-9/11 GI Bill, waiting to be used.

Having the financial means to earn a degree is a huge benefit and something you can use to your advantage. When you first leave the military, it may not be the best time for you to go to school, but within a year or two at the most, you should have established a plan for how you are going to get a primary or secondary degree. The sooner the better; putting it off out of fear is understandable but not a good excuse for long.

If you entered the military right after high school or even after a few semesters of college, then your schooldays may seem like light years ago. You may not feel that college is right for you, or you may not believe you are smart enough. But you can do it, and it is much easier than you think. If you have questions about your ability to earn a degree, know you are not the only veteran to doubt yourself. You would be surprised by how long it takes some to realize they can do this. And so can you. If you are confident about yourself and your getting an education, you should start the process immediately—before you leave the military so you are enrolled for the semester following your discharge.

To succeed in your educational goals, it's vital to determine which learning platform works best for you. It may be taking online classes or being an in-class student; only you know the answer. With the birth of the Internet and online learning, your options have really expanded in the last ten years, so the possibilities are endless for how you can get the degree you desire, whether it's through a university, college, junior college, technical school, or some other institution.

The bottom line is that education is an important part of the process for you moving forward. You need an education. It is so important, especially now when companies are requiring a bachelor's degree or, at minimum, an associate's degree for any entry-level positions that pay more than minimum wage. The steps outlined in this chapter are based on my firsthand knowledge of being exactly where you stand now. Let's get started!

7 Steps toward Your Educational Goals

1. Call the Veterans Affairs Education Benefits Line to find out your options based on your period of service.

2. Talk to your local Vocational Rehabilitation and Employment Center to verify your eligibility.

3. Meet with a VA or local state career counselor to determine your academic and educational goals.

4. Research the degree program you think will be a good match for you based on your career interests.

5. Find the right university or college to attend and apply for admission.

6. Apply for your VA Benefits and submit your FAFSA online to determine eligibility for both grants and loans.

7. Follow up with your veteran counselor and tie up any loose ends.

Step 1: Call the Veterans Affairs Education Benefits Line to Find Out Your Options Based on Your Period of Service

Based on your period of service, you may fall into one or several categories that entitle you to educational benefits. Understanding what these benefits are and how they can help you is a very important aspect of beginning your educational journey that will ultimately advance your current or future career.

Remember, if you do not ask, no one will tell you. That is why you have to ask appropriate questions to gain the information you need to make solid, fact-based decisions that will save you time and grief down the road. As you know from the military, there is no dumb question.

So do not be afraid to speak up at any point when it concerns benefits you are entitled to, based on the service and sacrifices you made for your country.

To connect with the VA Education and Training Department, the number you want to call, as of the time of this publication, is 1-888-442-4551. This phone call will provide you with a lot of information you will use to move forward with the other steps in this chapter. However, before calling, do some research so you understand the terminology within the GI Bill program and so you can gather any helpful information you will need during the call. That way, you will understand fully what your benefits are and how you will receive them.

You can do this research at the VA Education and Training Department's website (http://www.benefits.va.gov/gibill/index.asp at the time of this printing). This site is the main access point to learn about the GI Bill and specific options you may have. Other secondary websites you can use can be found through an Internet search or by consulting the resources section in the back of this book.

When you actually make the phone call, make sure you are free from distractions and you have pen and paper ready to take notes. Ask as many questions as you need to during your call. Don't forget to request that information be sent to you directly so you have it at your fingertips and it can direct you to other resources for any additional questions you may have. The key is to feel comfortable by making sure you understand everything. If you end up having to make a few phone calls because you forgot to ask something, that is okay. Just call back or do more research to ensure you are ready to move on to step 2.

Step 2: Talk to Your Local Vocational Rehabilitation and Employment Center to Verify Your Eligibility

Many programs assist both veterans and disabled veterans as they attempt to overcome barriers after returning home. The Department of Veterans Affairs has a program it offers called Vocational Rehabilitation and Employment (or VR&E for short), and veterans who meet a certain criteria have the ability to get job preparation, job assistance, employment accommodations, and educational assistance for free.

Vocational Rehabilitation and Employment is a great service you can use to learn more about your exact career goals and help with job placements.

To start off, the website is a great place to find out more about the program and receive answers to specific eligibility requirement questions you may have. After reviewing the website, it is probably a good idea to call VR&E and explain your particular situation so you get the proper guidance for how to proceed for any special cases, along with getting information on how to submit your application online. If you have further questions, call the Department of Veterans Affairs, 1-800-827-1000. After speaking with a representative, it is time to apply for the benefits through eBenefits. You can get there directly by going to the Vocational Rehabilitation and Employment website (http://www.benefits.va.gov/vocrehab/) and clicking on "Apply for Veterans Benefits via VONAPP" (Veterans Online Application). At that point, you can create an account so you can move forward with the application.

You may need to fill out up to three different forms, depending on the services you are applying for. You can fill them out online or print them and take them into your local VA Regional Office. The forms are:

- VA Form 28-1900: Everyone will need to fill out this form when applying for vocational rehabilitation.

- VA Form 28-0588: Fill out this form only if you are a service member who has a disability that began or became worse during active duty but you have not yet received a Service-Connected Disability Rating.

- VA Form 28-8832: This form must be filled out by veterans and service members to apply for educational vocational counseling at no cost to the veteran.

There are wait times associated with submitting the forms and receiving a response, so try to be patient and follow up with VR&E to ensure your paperwork was submitted and processes successfully.

This can be a lengthy process, but it is really worth your time to invest in your future by having all your bases covered regarding the benefits you can utilize. Working directly with a counselor to determine what options you have at your disposal and how specifically to maximize your opportunities is extremely important. College may be an option, career placement may be an option, and there may even be a combination of both options available to you depending on your individual situation. The great news is that whatever benefit you use, there is a program in place to help you move forward.

Step 3: Meet With a VA or Local State Career Counselor to Determine Your Academic and Educational Goals

The next step is very important on your road to achieving your educational goals. Before you start researching colleges or universities and specific programs that you may want to enroll in, you must first establish what your specific educational goals are. Everyone has individual interests and having a career that is aligned with your interests usually means more satisfaction in the workplace and beyond into your personal life as well You must determine what you would like to go to school for to ensure you are not wasting both your time and your VA benefits in the process.

In addition to considering your interests, evaluate the country's current economic demands to help drill down on a career that has a good balance in meeting your needs psychologically and financially. Ask yourself where is the need for people in the workforce and how will obtaining your degree align you with a career path that will make you employable and be beneficial to you and your family. You must consider all this to ensure you can use your degree upon graduating from college, graduate school, technical school, a PhD program, law school, or any other institution or program.

There are so many choices for receiving a degree or certification that you really need to take the time to think about your options. One of the best ways to help you narrow down your options and determine what you want to do is to meet with a VA or local career counselor. State agencies also have veteran resources at the county level that assist veterans with establishing educational and career goals.

Tapping into these resources will help you understand what skills you are looking to develop further. There are so many fields to pursue, and so many different skills are sharpened as a result of pursuing educational advancements. If you can narrow down your goals to one to three options, you will know exactly how to proceed. There are also exercises you can do to help you determine what your interests are if you are having a hard time narrowing down your list. State and federal government resources can assist you with determining your exact interests as well. In addition, as a veteran, you can access the Employment Center on the eBenefits website (https://www.ebenefits.va.gov/ebenefits/jobs) to get more information on employment resources and services. You can also take a piece of paper and write down all your interests and match them with degree programs you may be interested in.

Many benefits can also result from establishing a relationship with a career counselor. Once you enroll in a university, you can find a career counselor there as well whom you can work with to determine further your educational goals. There is always someone to talk to who wants to help a veteran become successful, especially in determining his or her exact field of study.

> **This is the fun part: setting up the road map that will lead you to your final destination of success.**

Step 4: Research the Degree Program You Think Will Be a Good Match for You Based on Your Career Interests

With this newfound information in hand, it is time to put the pieces of the puzzle together. Once you figure out what you are good at and what you would like to do in the future that could be profitable, you must choose an educational route that will meet both your individual goals and specific needs. Many options are available, and finding the right one is critical for successfully returning to school post-military.

Because universities and colleges have so many programs, and different requirements for you to be accepted into a program, the sooner you get started on the process, the better. You will also need to meet application deadlines so there is no time to wait. You want to find out as much as possible about your area of interest so you lose no time getting into a program and don't end up having to wait for a year or more. This is especially true if the program you want to enter is a very specialized field of study that has only one entry point into the program during a particular time of the year. You also have to consider what test may be applicable for particular programs. Some tests that might be required, for example, are the LSAT for law school or the GRE or GMAT for graduate school. In order to meet the school's application deadlines, you may also have to meet the deadlines for any applicable exams.

You should create a checklist for each program and ensure that all deadlines are met on time to avoid any letdowns from not being diligent.

There are usually fees for each test, but your GI Bill or Post-9/11 GI Bill can help cover some of them. You should check with the education component of the VA to learn what paperwork is necessary if you go down that road, or you can pay out of pocket for the exam.

If you have a plan and follow it, everything will fall into place. But if you miss a window for one reason or another, you may have to consider another school or the next time to enroll.

Deciding on the right path and putting a great plan in place now will save you a lot of time and energy down the road.

With all the information you have gathered, you should have a pretty good idea of what schools you want to apply to and how they align with your specific interests, so you can be prepared.

Step 5: Find the Right University or College to Attend and Apply for Admission

Now that you have researched the schools with programs you are interested in, it is time to begin the application process.

Narrow down your list of schools to three and apply to them to ensure you get into a program you definitely want to be in. Hopefully, you will get into the school of your primary choice, but if not, you will have a backup that either you can live with or you can make a decision if you want to go another route.

The most important aspect to remember is that you need to be excited about whatever program you decide to enter. Otherwise, all the work you are doing now may end up being for nothing, or you may end up switching programs, which will result in extra work later. Look carefully at the requirements, course of study, and application for the program so you do not find yourself surprised or unhappy down the road. Many people have not taken these critical steps, so they end up dropping out of school or earning degrees or certifications they are not even using. You don't want to waste your precious benefits or your time and energy on anything less than the program and school that you believe meets your needs and desires. Your interests may change once you are in the college setting, but initially, you should have a good understanding of what your strengths and weaknesses are and the practicality of the program you are entering for your future career.

A final point to consider is, out of the three schools you are applying to, what is the relationship you will form with the university upon graduation? What are the alumni like, and is the school an accredited school? If you change schools and your credits will not transfer, that could be a major problem that will cost you valuable time and money.

You want to know everything about the school you finally choose to attend upon acceptance. You want to know how the veterans programs are run and supported, what paperwork needs to be submitted and maintained as a veteran, what specific programs are offered for veterans at the school, and also what the career services will do for you upon graduation to help you get placed in your field of study or advise you on furthering your education. Having this knowledge in place when you need it is equally as important as being accepted and receiving high marks during your time in school.

Step 6: Apply for Your VA Benefits and Submit Your FAFSA Online to Determine Eligibility for Both Grants and Loans

You are getting closer and closer to your goal of attending college or the school of your choice. Your next step is to file for benefits with the VA Education and Training Department for the school you have been accepted into. There are four ways you can apply based on information obtained from the US Department of Veterans Affairs website (Aug 2014):

- Apply online through the Veterans Online Application or VONAPP system at https://vabenefits.vba.va.gov/vonapp/default.asp.

- Visit your nearest VA regional office to apply in person.

- Consult with the VA certifying official—who is usually in the Registrar's or Financial Aid office—at the school of your choice. This official has application forms and can help you apply.

- Call 1-888-GI BILL-1 (1-888-442-4551) to have the application mailed to you.

Once you have submitted your application, both you and the school will be notified of the amount of the award, how it will be dispersed, and the remaining balance for the number of years of education to come, depending on the benefit you applied for. You can follow up with your school veteran representative to ensure that everything went through on the school's end and that it also filed for your benefits. It is a pretty smooth process when you stay active and involved in the process with both the VA and the school that accepted you.

The money from the VA may go directly to the school, or it may go directly to you, depending on the type of benefit you receive. You may also be eligible for a monthly stipend, as either an online or an in-class student, to help cover your expenses, such as room and board or schoolbooks. The rates may vary, so be sure to read your award letter for clarification.

You should also follow up with the VA for any clarification on benefits you are entitled to that you do not understand or that are not mentioned in your award letter.

The next step after you have secured the money through your GI Bill or your Post-9/11 GI Bill is to get your loans and grants approved through FAFSA (Free Application for Federal Student Aid). You can and should apply for these benefits at the same time that you apply for your VA benefits. You have to go on the FAFSA website (https://fafsa.ed.gov) to create a login and apply. In addition, you need your previous tax year information, and if your parents claimed you as a dependent, you need their tax information to complete all of the necessary fields in the application.

You will get an email response to confirm your application has been received, followed by one stating it has been processed. Then you will get an award letter from the school explaining what your grant and loan amounts are, based on your field of study and prospective degree.

Now that you have completed both of these applications, you are almost set to begin classes, which is very exciting after all the steps you have taken to get to this point.

Step 7: Follow Up With Your Veteran Counselor and Tie Up Any Loose Ends

After you have gotten confirmation that all your submissions are processed and you are all set up through both the Department of Veterans Affairs and your university or school of choice, you are ready to go. Reach out to either a mentor you have been working with or your veteran counselor through Vocational Rehab or your school to continue the conversation and ensure that everything is lined up for your start date of classes. Work with your counselor closely through your transition, and allow those around you to do their jobs so you can concentrate on what you need to.

If anything is outstanding in terms of additional necessary paperwork, ensure you get it completed in time so it does not delay your entry into the program you are starting. Make sure you order the necessary books for class ahead of time, and also make sure that you have a copy of the syllabus for your courses. Knowing what to expect ahead of time can really make a difference once classes begin.

★ ★ ★

You have accomplished quite a bit over the course of your life, and now, the latest chapter is about to begin. This should be a very exciting time for you, though it could also be very stressful. Starting new classes and entering a new environment can be terrifying, especially as a veteran. Keep faith in yourself and your ability to overcome, no matter the obstacle in your way.

You will succeed in this chapter of your life, and even if you fall, you will be better equipped to get back up all the quicker. The sacrifices are worthwhile in the long run, and you will prevail. Even if it takes a little bit longer than you originally thought, that is okay. This is not a race. You must go through your educational advancements at your own pace and at the level you feel comfortable.

No one else is you or could ever be you. You are unique and brave. You have served your country, and now you are in the process of accepting life after the military. Be proud of who you are and your accomplishments. As a veteran, people along your journey will help you have success, but others may not. Holding resentment or anger does not help, and understanding the realities of life is a good practice. You have to set goals for yourself and work to put yourself in the best position to have success, no matter what.

Bottom line: Life is hard, but you can do anything you put your mind to.

Good luck!

Chapter 6
Creating Connections through Networking

Every job opportunity I have had in my life came about from a veteran connection I created and developed during my post-military career. My ability to get involved with people and organizations face to face has had a direct impact on my life in so many ways. If I had not made these key veteran connections and networked effectively, I would not have reached the level of success I have attained in my life. I was meant to meet the people I sought to meet; those specific people have positively impacted my life beyond comprehension. Without my hard work, perseverance, and direct communication with both friends and strangers, I would have missed opportunities that have forever changed my life.

The people you know are the people who will help shape your future into whatever you want it to be. With that in mind, the more people you know, the more opportunities you will have throughout your life. The key is creating wholesome relationships, not only with other veterans but also with civilians and the individuals in key positions who are going to expand further the base of prospects you have within your reach and beyond.

When you have a network of people in your corner, you are setting yourself up for success in every way possible. Nothing happens overnight, but in time, the people who are meant to be in your life will be the ones who help determine your future. However, you must invest both your time and energy with them in a very productive way for both of you to have positive results in the relationship. You have to give in order to receive, and it takes a true commitment to show you are equally invested in growing a real partnership that has mutual benefits.

People will help you in the transitioning phase from the military into civilian life if you take the initiative to go beyond the casual everyday interactions of life. You must establish a level of sincerity that projects your true intentions the majority of the time. People always know when they are being used, and no one likes to waste time with people who are takers more than givers.

Sincerity is a key asset when trying to transform your social network from just being on the Internet into real-life, effective, and mutually beneficial interactions.

What makes a difference is not necessarily the phone call someone can make or the email someone can write on your behalf. It is the trust and faith in your abilities that someone has when making a recommendation on your behalf. When someone steps up to the plate to recommend you, that person needs to know you are going to deliver because the individual is putting his or her own reputation at risk. This is a big deal and should be taken very seriously. People will not put their stamp on you unless you take the time to build a foundation that makes them believe in you and your capabilities in a professional and personal setting.

7 Steps toward Building Your Network

1. Conduct research to determine the target outcome of your professional connections.
2. Create a LinkedIn account, and set yourself up with a professional-looking page.
3. Connect with all your family and friends.
4. Reach out to all military contacts past and present to establish a Web of Veterans United for Success.
5. Link up with veterans organizations such as Disabled American Veterans and the American Legion to make new connections.
6. Leverage your network through social media.
7. Be diligent and follow up with all connections as you begin to foster real long-term relationships.

Step 1: Conduct Research to Determine the Target Outcome of Your Professional Connections

As you are making professional connections, you have to keep a cool demeanor and have clear objectives with every single person you meet. The timing of a true professional connection that could help you is very valuable. If you bring value to the table and have something to offer in exchange for someone else's professional friendship, you will be in the club, so to speak. If you waste the person's time and babble on and on about something that offers little or no value to the person, he or she will blow you off.

It is that simple. If you do not catch the person's attention in the few minutes you two are speaking, he or she will act interested but will really be thinking about where happy hour is later. Sure, you may get a business card or the verbal mention of a follow-up call or email, but it will never come unless you give the person an actual reason to do so. Here is where your preparation has to come shining through. You have to know everything about the individual you are trying to gain access to so that when you present yourself, you are doing so with a fully loaded weapon of knowledge.

There are two types of professional connections: a business acquaintance and a decision maker. A business acquaintance is someone you see every so often or are casually connected with on social media as an indication of knowing one another. A decision maker is not your friend in the true sense of the word; rather, he or she is your golden ticket to a breakthrough opportunity in your life, personally and professionally.

The people you meet in your life are not random; you can get yourself into the room of a key person who will help you if you want it badly enough.

Now how do you get in the same room with the decision maker, who is the primary focus of energy towards your goal? Is it through social media? Is it through phone contacts to his or her office? The answer is through direct communication. That usually is face to face, but if physical distance creates a barrier, optional methods can be used to increase your chances of becoming an ally of this substantial connection. Before you get all excited and try to contact this person immediately, it is best to map out a plan of action for how you will do so.

Here is where the meat and potatoes of your research begins. If you fail to do the proper research and fail to define what you want from this individual, you will likely not be very successful in your quest. However, if you uncover every rock, connect the dots, and act professionally in your delivery, you will have success. Sometimes even having someone on the inside who can put the word out there for you, before you even meet this person, could make the meeting that much more successful on game day. The power to change your life is in your hands, and it starts with aligning yourself with people who have a vested interest in your success.

Step 2: Create a LinkedIn Account, and Set Yourself Up with a Professional-Looking Page

After determining what your goals and objectives are, it is time to establish your "face" in the public eye. Like it or not, social media and the Internet have taken over and are here to stay. The world we all live in has been evolving at a rapid pace with the technological advancements that have taken place over the past fifteen years. With that being said, on social media, everyone can view what you have done and how you did it in the blink of an eye. Quite frankly, nothing is private anymore, so the sooner you adapt to this environment, the better.

Many tutorials and best practices are available on the Internet and in print for understanding the ins and outs of LinkedIn so you can use it in the most effective manner to accomplish your goals. Please consult those resources because I will not go into the details of how to perfect your page here. Let me just give you an overview of the most important elements. The basic requirements to get started are a profile picture, a list of accomplishments, educational background information, and employment history. The most important thing to remember in using LinkedIn is that the more time you put into it, the more effective you will be in reaching your goals.

For your profile picture, you want to have a professional photo or a high quality headshot so people can see you in your element, whatever that may be. Your identity is established with this photo, and others will judge you based on what they see. This may not seem fair, but it is the truth, unfortunately. Everyone should be judged on his or her knowledge, skills, and abilities, first and foremost. However, we all know that many people still judge a book by its cover.

LinkedIn is your first opportunity to get face to face with someone you would like to meet or have met previously. Unlike Facebook, where you may be trying to gather friends for the sake of having a "number count," at LinkedIn, you want to create a network of trusted associates who will go to bat for you when you need them most. It is far more valuable to have one hundred close friends than ten thousand connections. No one really cares how many friends or connections you have. People want to know whether you will deliver on what you say you will do, whether you are trustworthy, and whether you add value to their lives.

As a veteran or disabled veteran, you want to showcase your skills to deliver and be accountable. Your background is the perfect place to start when you configure your page and the content you will include on it. It is a blank sheet of paper right now, and you are the one who will fill in the blanks with your specific information. Lying or exaggerating your background or accomplishments is a great way to destroy your bridge before it is built; it will also distance you from people who can help you reach your goals.

Present the best you in the most truthful way possible, and you will be noticed before you know it!

Step 3: Connect with All Your Family and Friends

The greatest allies you have are those already in your inner circle, including your family and friends. They hold the keys to the castle and are the easiest connections to tap into. In most cases, all you have to do is ask, and they will help. How many times have you just bought a new car or something else, only to have someone say to you after the fact, "I wished you would have asked me because I know just the right person who could have helped you"? It is that simple.

Getting over the fear or embarrassment you may have about asking someone else for help is step 1. This is a common and understandable feeling, especially for veterans because we have been trained to be independent and rely on our instincts to get through pressure situations. However, in the civilian world, we all need each other, so reaching out to our closest friends gives us the best insider information on the market.

This is true because other people may know about job opportunities you will never find out about, or they can put in a good word for you that allows you to get through the screening process without being grouped together with the other fifty to one thousand applicants. This connection is your liquid gold. You need your friends and family now more than ever.

The job-seeking process can take anywhere from six months to a year, if not longer.

Time is of the essence, and having a flawed process could put you into a financial hole that greatly impacts many areas of your life.

Obviously, our jobs are the single-most important tool for our survival because without a job or income to support ourselves and our families, we are swimming against the current, which is no fun at all. No veteran should lose his car or home because he did not use the most important asset at his disposal.

The best way to approach the situation is to have a good attitude and be professional. When you ask a friend for assistance, make sure you highlight your strengths and explain the specific position for which you want to be considered. There is no sense in asking someone to help you get an interview for a position you don't even want. This is a waste of time and will upset many people in the process. Remember, the person referring you is putting his or her credibility on the line for you. Put your best foot forward and be appreciative for every opportunity that presents itself to you, whether it is a good fit for you or not.

Step 4: Reach Out to All Military Contacts Past and Present to Establish a Web of Veterans United for Success

This step is one of the most fun in the book because you get to connect in an entirely different way with soldiers you know. Your battle buddies to your left and right over the years probably know you better than anyone on Earth, except maybe your mother. We create relationships as thick as blood in the service, and these bonds are easier to maintain than ever before.

Prior to the Information Age, soldiers did not have LinkedIn or Facebook to connect with each other. Now you can, in real time, connect on the spot with someone and have access to his or her entire professional work history and connections to use for your benefit. Guess what the best part is about this. Your colleagues want to help you succeed. Your fellow veterans cannot wait to help you get a job. You were their bunk mate in basic training, and how would they have gotten by without your mom's chocolate chip cookies? People remember what you do for them, and hopefully, you left a good impression because your reputation is all you have in this world.

Your friends will go beyond what you can individually achieve in helping you to seek a high-quality employment opportunity. The connections you establish may or may not help you today, but in the future, they can and most likely will greatly impact another veteran you may not even know at this point, and that feeling of having helped another is beneficial in itself. This Web of Veterans United for Success is how we can all give back to those who have served our country, just as someone might be assisting you right now. It is a simple concept, and it begins with you reaching your goals, which are aligned with the goals of countless veterans around the country.

Once you have reached out to those people in the military community who have your back, it is time to get down to business. It is time to set up meetings that are either in person or virtual to come up with a game plan for how you will separate yourself from the thousands and thousands of non-veteran applicants. You have transferable skills; you just need to figure out how to use those skills so, like with a .50 caliber, you make the greatest center mass hits possible.

The application and hiring process is a challenge centered on finding the best way to get your name in front of the hiring manager without being screened out. Knowing how to fill out the application is an aspect that other veterans who are your friends can help you navigate; they can especially help by letting you know what worked for them in terms of converting military jargon to transferable skills on your resume to strengthen your application as a veteran. You are in great hands, and before you know it, you will be owing your military friends a big thank-you for helping you move forward either in an interview or by connecting you with someone who can help you.

Step 5: Link Up with Veterans Organizations Such as Disabled American Veterans and the American Legion to Make New Connections

Many organizations support veterans, whether they are for-profit or non-profit companies, and many have their own assistance programs. It will be critical for your success, therefore, to do some initial research to identify the veterans group that offers the platform that will give you the biggest return for your time invested. This return on investment may or may not come from solely one organization. You may have to choose a few companies to help you fill your bucket with the necessary items to be time on target, or TOT.

For example, if you want to focus on your benefits with the Veterans Administration, you may choose one organization to help you prepare your documentation and get your medical records in order. If you are looking for involvement with other like-minded veterans, you may choose to get involved with another organization. If you want to start a business as a veteran and need more information and/or training, you may go with another veteran entity. You decide on the map to follow since you have the keys to the vehicle you are driving—your life.

Many people love veterans and want to help you succeed, but it is important to weed out those organizations that do not align with where you want to go.

It is equally important to know that, although one company does not fit your needs today, it may well be of value to you later.

This is the fun and interesting part of your transition. You get to decide who will help you and how. It is easy to become bogged down in this process, but when you ask, doors will open.

The worst thing someone can say to you is no, and that may just be a temporary no. Persistence is key as you align with veteran groups and stay aware of the direction they are going to afford veterans' opportunities. It shouldn't take long to figure out whether a veterans' organization is in existence for the right reasons or just caught up in the hype, without actually making a difference for the men and women who need it the most. You want to stay away from organizations that are all talk and no action.

On the flip side, aligning yourself with valuable groups is key to your next opportunity or quality-of-life improvement. You will be amazed by the results that can come about from relationships formed with people who love veterans and are very appreciative for our sacrifices. The next person you meet through one of these organizations could end up being your mentor or know someone who knows of a great job that would be perfect for your skill set or become your next business partner for a new product or service that you believe will be profitable. You never know what can happen, and when you seek, you shall find, more times than not.

Step 6: Leverage Your Network through Social Media

Today, social media has become a way of life for a global economy of people trying to stay connected. We must all accept that the companies who help us do so are most likely here to stay, and before we know it, everything is going to be digital. The people you know are the ones most likely to impact your life, along with those you add to your network through your interactions with organizations and people you meet daily. The truth is that we are all connected, and we need each other to meet our financial obligations.

Being able to communicate and use electronic means to develop a sophisticated network of people you can trust will make all the difference in the world.

It is not always what you know but whom you know that leads to success. Making daily strategic posts to gain attention for the right professional reasons will naturally attract people into your circle who see value in what you have to offer. Social media is becoming the gateway to all our futures. You may think this good or bad, but it is a reality and vital for our future survival in our ever-evolving world.

Your character and how you are perceived are the keys to your professional career; how you are viewed and the credentials you have really matter in the digital age. People can quickly have access to your professional and personal story if you put it out for everyone to view because almost everyone has access to a computer and search engines such as Google. Nothing is really private anymore, so you have to be aware of what you put out into the world for others to see. If you are unaware of the balance between social media and your career, you are in for a huge wakeup call. You do not want to be a victim of a blunder that costs you an opportunity because of what someone finds out about you on the Internet.

Your posts on social media should be aligned with the goals you have for yourself as a professional. These posts should be both informative and attract the right kind of attention to your profile on platforms such as LinkedIn, Twitter, and Facebook as a launching pad to your success. This process is going to take time unless you are a celebrity, in the media spotlight for the work you are doing, or have an interesting story, product, or service that brings you to the forefront of people's minds. That is the ultimate goal: to be relevant and attract the right kind of attention that allows you to go further than ever before by leveraging the people who know who you are.

The times have changed; people used to stay with companies for twenty or thirty years. Nowadays, people are making moves constantly, and companies are looking for talent to replace what is lost in a world where there is not enough talent to go around. You can be that candidate who gets recruited and maybe that breath of fresh air a company is looking for to move it forward. The skills you gained in the military can be critical for meeting the needs of those requiring that level of expertise. Shaping your network to your benefit will reap rewards sooner rather than later if you are smart in your approach to what social media can actually mean for you as a veteran back in the civilian sector attempting to take positive steps forward.

Step 7: Be Diligent and Follow Up with All Connections as You Begin to Foster Real Long-Term Relationships

As you progress further, you will begin to realize the results of your labors are starting to come together. It may not happen as fast as you would like in some cases, but it will eventually happen. Sometimes we have to have patience and stay diligent in our efforts. This can be easier said than done. However, if you give up, you will never know what could have been. Your life can change in the matter of one day or a few hours. That is how fragile life is when you sit back and think about it.

You never know when a person you met will come through on your behalf or whether you will meet someone today or tomorrow who is the key to your success. You have to stay sharp and bend your mind in positive ways you never thought possible to get what you have worked so hard for. As you build trust with those around you, you will start to see a difference in the little battles—in fact, you will start to win them over time. It could happen lightning quick, or it could take some time. It just depends on the timing of life, the people you meet, and how you manage your time in developing and executing an effective plan.

The biggest lesson to be learned is to realize the value in other people and to understand that we all need each other. If you make connections for the wrong reasons, those people will not give you the time of day in return. Your approach has to show that you care about the individual you are working with and that you have something of value to offer in exchange for having your needs met. When you work well with others and show concern for them, your networking will be that much more productive.

Another point to remember is that other people have their own lives and their own goals they are working toward. If you do not stay on top of your game, the connections you make will pass you by; they will move on to other people more aligned with their goals. If you can get some time with someone going in the same direction as you, you need to embrace that person and ride the wave home. There is a technical aspect to what you are trying to accomplish, and as you master your skills, you will become more fluid in your approach. As you learn, you may have fears about failure, but remember that even if you fail in one approach, that does not mean another well-thought-out approach will not succeed.

★ ★ ★

You must look at things from a new perspective as a veteran who is striving for excellence, or maybe as someone who just wants to provide for his or her family. We all have our individual reasons for why we do what we do and why we are motivated in the individual and unique ways we are. Stay on top of your craft, keep reaching for the stars, and follow up with every connection you make. You never know how far you can go unless you stretch toward the objective in your mind.

Chapter 7
Starting a Business as a Vetrepreneur

Upon leaving the military in late 2001, I never could have imagined that I would start a veteran-owned business (Power of One, LLC) as a vetrepreneur over ten years later. In fact, I never would have thought that I would be a published author, either. The skills I gained in the military have afforded me the building blocks and essential tools needed not only for my professional career as a civilian but also to reach the highest pinnacle of my goals as a business owner.

Believe it or not, having served in the military has given you skills you do not even realize you have. When it comes to launching and operating a business, you are in possession of the most valuable tools any school or institution could teach you at an entry level. Sure, there is information and specific technical knowledge you will need to gain as you move forward if you choose to start your own business, but there is nothing you cannot accomplish based on what you learned in the US military, regardless of the branch you were in or the type of service you provided to your country.

Realizing that you have the essential building blocks of business in areas such as teamwork, organizational skills, time management, and budgeting means that you could really have great financial rewards down the road if you choose to become a vetrepreneur. But to do so, you need a well-thought-out business plan, high-quality resources, startup cash, an action plan, and the mettle to succeed, even if you fail or lose money to begin with. Your focus needs to be on not the potential short-term losses but, rather, the long-term plans that must come to fruition. Your success depends on your ability to persevere and go further than anyone ever thought possible, despite the obstacles you may face.

To succeed as a vetrepreneur, you need a unique idea that meets a need or solves a problem. This idea will be in the form of a product or service you will provide to your customers. The niche you make will ultimately lead to brand awareness on a local or global scale, depending on the size of your vision for yourself. You can dream as big as you want, and no one can stop you—except you—from reaching the goals you set if you make the decision to proceed with your ideas, whether they are currently in a beginning or advanced state.

Of course, we all can use some inspiration or motivation when we set a goal. There are specific steps you can take to help you realize the validity of the direction you want to go. Realize that the business you start may not be the business you end up making money on, so be flexible, and adapt to the global and economic market around you. As a vetrepreneur, you constantly have to deal with change. Being a business owner or company president is not just about having a fancy title. It also means you have to create results, track your finances, find customers, and create a work culture for your employees.

The sky is the limit, and the future is yours as a vetrepreneur if you choose to go down that road.

If so, this chapter will provide you with valuable information to assist you in this endeavor as a pioneer or trendsetter in the industry of your choice.

7 Steps Toward Establishing Your Business

1. Formulate an idea for a product or service that can solve a problem, satisfy a need, or achieve a specific goal.

2. Identify the exact industry or industries in which you want to conduct operations.

3. Speak to other veteran business owners.

4. Write a business plan and have it reviewed by a professional for feasibility.

5. Set realistic short- and long-term goals for your business income.

6. Organize the business's structure and make the necessary business connections that will align your company for success.

7. Start raising the capital and file all necessary company-related documents.

Step 1: Formulate an Idea for a Product or Service That Can Solve a Problem, Satisfy a Need, or Achieve a Specific Goal

Starting a business is a journey with many ups and downs. You may have an idea for a business that you know is going to have impacts, but you are not sure how you can make it happen on a limited budget or without the resources available to commit to your dreams. You would be surprised by what you can do when your back is against the wall. Being a veteran has its advantages; you have so many resources at your disposal that you may want to look into before you discount whether starting your own business is the right course of action for you.

Have you put your idea on paper, or have you discussed your thoughts with a colleague? How much planning has gone into this idea so far? Is it the right time to move ahead with your idea at this point in your life? Do you have any obstacles in your way that could prevent you from putting your thoughts into actions?

After you have spent some real time formalizing your thoughts, you need to determine whether your business is viable. Will it be something that customers want? There are three fundamental questions to ask yourself before you put further energy into your idea:

1. Does your idea solve a problem?
2. Does your idea satisfy a need?
3. Does your idea achieve a specific goal?

You will not be successful unless you can answer these questions in a positive, comprehensive, and well-thought-out manner. In order to have a business, you need customers; if you're not providing a product or service people want, your business won't last very long. Having an idea is one thing. Understanding the building blocks of how to bring that idea to market and make it viable will save you thousands of dollars, countless hours of wasted time, and endless disappointment if your plan fails. Do not be afraid to write down your responses to these very important questions and continually return to them and revise them as your focus for your business becomes clearer.

Once your plan is on paper, you own it, and moving forward, you are in control of what happens next. Being in business is not about the intent; rather, it is about the results. Many people have had ideas that have grown out of a garage into a global commodity, while others have invested everything they have into something that did not work out the way they originally thought. Failure is not an option if you choose to go down this road; through careful thought and by refining your idea as needed, you may have the potential to create a business that is needed.

The rest of the process depends on your ability to follow your plan through from A to B. You have the training. You have the skillset. You have the ability to learn and adapt as you move closer to your objective. Keep this in mind, and do not be afraid to put in the work that could end up making a difference to someone who believes in what you have to offer as much as you do.

Step 2: Identify the Exact Industry or Industries in Which You Want to Conduct Operations

One of the most important aspects of business is knowing exactly where you will operate and what your specific niche within your industry will be. Forecasting and projections go a long way, but without a point of reference as a new business owner, you will have to rely on market trends and your individual research, along with substantial data you will have to gather in order to get the biggest bang for your buck. Having a team in place to help you identify these opportunities is the ideal circumstance.

You most likely have a million questions, and the first one on your mind will be, "Who will buy my product or want to use the services I provide?" In addition, will those buyers be local, national, or international customers? What is the demographic area that your strategic plan will operate in? Having the ability to connect with people in your industry will go a long way toward reducing your learning curve as a business owner.

Once you know the area of focus for your product or service, dig deep past the surface to identify successful strategies you can use to make your business idea a reality.

Being able to identify what you could do better than a competitor will equally allow you to formulate ideas that can shape the foundation of what is to come. That is why you should establish a solid mission and vision for what you believe in, which will in turn help you lay the bricks in a manner that fits the model you are developing.

With ever-changing markets and economies, consumers' needs and wants are changing at a rapid pace. Changing with the times, anticipating trends, and identifying ways to be very innovative are all ways to get things off the ground for the long-term. But to do that, you have to make the short-term plans a reality while being careful not to bite off more than you can handle. Every battle you can win will lead to the goal of meeting your objective in the least amount of time possible. It takes a calculated effort to get your plans off the ground.

If you are in the defense industry, you should work to maximize your veteran network, which we will discuss shortly. If you are in the research and development industry, you can link up with universities, major corporations, and other startups to work on projects in line with what you are doing. So many potential scenarios exist that only you, as the founder, can truly identify what will be a good match for your business. Gather information that will help you imagine the big picture of what your business will look like when it is truly successful; keep that big picture in mind, and chart a course that will eventually turn it into a reality.

Step 3: Speak to Other Veteran Business Owners
The primary goal of many veteran programs is to help those previously called to serve their country to start, operate, and succeed as a business owner. Such programs include the En-

trepreneurship Bootcamp for Veterans National Program (EBV) and Entrepreneurship Bootcamp for Veterans' Families (EBV-F). Certain requirements must be met to attend these programs. To find out more about them, visit http://ebv.vets. syr.edu for the EBV National Program and http://ebv.vets.syr. edu/families/ for the EBV-F.

These programs and others lay the foundation for turning an idea into a reality. One benefit of going through a business program for veterans is the interaction you get to have with other veterans who have similar dreams or are starting to put their plans into action as startup business owners. These people can be great sources of information for you as you begin to learn the ropes of what it takes to be successful.

People who have succeeded in establishing a business can help you with answering your numerous questions, whether it is giving you ideas on how to raise money or sharing the steps to gain legal protection for your company through copyrights or trademark filings. Whatever question or situation you're facing, there's likely another veteran who can lead you in the right direction, based on his or her experiences. If you do not ask questions, how will you ever find the answers?

People may come into your life at the exact moment you need them, but you also have to put yourself in situations where you can meet the people who can help you.

The ins and outs of business can be complex or simple if you have an effective formula for implementing your strategy. Usually, there will be many days of trial and error that can be very time-consuming and cost you a lot of money; however, with the help of other veterans who are willing to share their stories and experiences, you can limit the number of mistakes you make. Identify the strengths your veteran colleagues bring to their customers and identify their weaknesses as well; all this information or data is obtainable if you put in the effort. Most veterans will be happy to give you their time if you are sincere in your desire to use your military experiences for something positive in this world that you are very passionate about.

Step 4: Write a Business Plan and Have It Reviewed by a Professional for Feasibility

Having a complete and thorough business plan is an essential part of getting your idea off the ground.

Having a poorly put-together plan will hinder most entrepreneurs from reaching their full potential.

Creating a good business plan can be a difficult process, especially if it is your first one. However, with the right amount of thought and innovation, you could produce a working product that is successful. There are several components to a business plan, and leaving out a critical element could set you back in terms of time and money very quickly.

Business plans come in many versions, and you can find numerous examples on the Internet or in business books as a starting point for you. The main components are:

- Executive summary
- Business description and vision
- Definition of your market
- A core target-marketing and sales strategy
- Organizational structure
- Financial management with realistic projections and forecasts based on in-depth market analysis

Your business idea needs to take shape in a realistic and visible way, which happens when you perfect the process from step to step in your plan.

You will have many versions of the plan as it develops over time. Being able to articulate and substantiate what you want to do is vital to the plan actually working. Projections are just that. There are no guarantees in business, but the more valid your information, the better your success rate will likely be. If you start with a two-hundred-thousand-dollar investment and no real plan, you could be out two hundred thousand dollars in a relatively short period.

Good decision making and a firm definition of your idea is critical. Equally important are the connections and relationships you form. Many a business started in a garage and became a household name over time. It can happen to you, and it will if you invest some real thought and time into your idea.

Once you have created your business plan, ask for outside input on the feasibility of what you are doing. Talk to industry leaders and other advisers you currently have in your corner. If you cannot understand your own plan, usually someone else won't either. That is why when professionals review your plan, they usually will give you advice on how you can further define what you are doing, or they will let you know you are ready to move forward because they believe you have a winning formula.

Step 5: Set Realistic Short- and Long-Term Goals for Your Business Income

Prior to launching your business, do some planning on where monies will be allocated once the company starts to gain revenue. You will always have your fixed operating costs—expenses for the operation of the business that are continuous on a month-to-month basis. Knowing those costs upfront is very important for keeping your budget on track. When it comes to surpluses and growth, you equally have to know where the funds will be distributed in order to maximize company profitability and growth in both the short-term and long-term.

The main goal of any business is to stay profitable while delivering a high quality product or service that will meet consumer demand. So the thought process initially is: How can I meet my customers' needs now while also preparing to provide what they will need in the future? Growth is only possible when funds are properly allocated, which happens through adequate research and development.

If revenue is coming in, but it is not being used properly, the company could end up failing in the long term. Many companies try to dog-paddle to stay afloat, instead of taking calculated business risks that will produce results and take the business further toward the founder's original vision. Supporting information and data help determine if the reward is worth the risk. Sometimes these risks go as planned, and sometimes they do not. The goal is to have done adequate research and enough quality planning to give you a greater likelihood of being successful beyond the quarterly balance sheet.

Having a vision that aligns with the work being done day-to-day will make the growth process easier.

If there is no direct plan for a company's growth, it will continue to stay on the same path while its competitors learn and grow to meet their vision for their companies, while also gaining support from customers that used to be yours. Because it is a highly competitive market, short-term success does not guarantee long-term success.

Setting goals and working toward them will not only allow you to stay ahead of competitors, but it will also allow your business to gain recognition as an industry leader. Being on the forefront of change is always better than being two steps behind. Your business's ability to create revenue and grow will determine how long it is successful. Most new businesses fail in the first two to three years due to their inability to stay relevant or because they are delivering an inept product or service.

Step 6: Organize the Business's Structure and Make the Necessary Business Connections That Will Align Your Company for Success

Once you have a vision and strategy for your business, you need to determine its organizational structure; then you will know who will carry out which processes so everything works seamlessly. Many people think that winging it works here. However, when that approach is taken, valuable resources, time, and money are squandered.

Knowing who does what and when will make your life much easier, regardless of how many employees you have. Most startups have only a few employees or begin as a one-person operation. In those situations, you might think it is unimportant to have a structure because of limited resources; however, it is equally important, if not more important, to have a strategy in place that allows you to control what work is being completed on a daily basis. In addition, contacting an accountant and business attorney is a good idea to establish the needed guidance in shaping the perimeters of your business.

When you have structure, you have a plan, but when you lack structure, your ability to complete tasks that allow you to be successful will be negatively affected. Once you know who is doing what and when, then as your business starts to grow, you can explore the endless possibilities coming at you from different directions. At first, it may seem as if you will never get your idea off the ground, but when the train starts moving, it really starts to move.

You have to be selective about which customers you want to align with because not all customers are good customers. You want to strive for high quality in the products and services

you provide while also concentrating on top-quality customers who will be loyal and forgiving when you make mistakes.

**Getting in front of the right business connections and
making the right decisions for whom to collaborate with on
projects will make a significant difference in your business.**

In most cases, your business will need employees who
can network in order for it to operate efficiently. Empowering
others to ensure your business is successful takes planning and
finesse. You must know how to get your product or service to
the end user with the least cost possible without compromis-
ing your business's integrity. Operating a successful business
is a complex process. It takes a lot of work and effort to realize
your full potential, so having trusted and dependable allies
can make your road map to success much clearer.

Step 7: Start Raising the Capital and File All Necessary Company-Related Documents

You can get the funding you need for your business in many
different ways. Depending on how much money you need,
family and friends are often a good place to start. Even if they
can't offer you financial support, they will give you mental and
emotional support and help generate excitement that you are
actually going to go for it. With this excitement comes a great
level of respect and a desire to help you become successful. Most
people around you are in your corner, and they really want to
see you succeed; even those who may not be able to help, probably would if they could. It's good to have people in your corner,
regardless of how much they can commit to helping you.

If you need more money than you can generate from
your family and friends, a small business loan can help. You
can also get backing for a loan, in some cases, from the Small
Business Association. In addition, venture capitalists are always looking for the next big thing to invest in, so they may

be another viable option. Many people have even taken out personal loans, utilized their own savings, or put some startup costs on personal credit cards to get their businesses going.

There is a fine line between going dangerously into debt for your business and taking educated financial risks to help it come to fruition.

It is best to speak with your legal and tax consultants before you make any final decisions on how your business will be financed. Having a good business plan will most likely lead to less financial waste.

Once you have the funding and have worked out the financial details, it is time to file the necessary papers for the state you are in, along with any specialized licenses, federal licenses, if applicable, and trademark and copyright filings that may be applicable to protect your ideas, intellectual property, and business as a whole. Again, having your attorney's involvement will ensure that you are legally crossing all the t's and dotting all the i's. Once you have done this, all your hard work should start to pay off.

★ ★ ★

I personally wish you the best of luck if being a vetrepreneur is the path you choose to follow. Being a business owner will provide you an opportunity to wake up every day and seize the opportunities all around you in order to make changes that are profound in your life. You can light a flame for others to follow and also set a path for your individual life moving forward.

It is not the change that makes the man but, rather, the man that makes the changes necessary to move beyond the uncertainties of life.
— Michael Bluemling Jr.

Chapter 8
Find Your Passion, Stay Dedicated, and Keep Climbing

I appreciate the opportunity I have had in these pages to share my experiences and knowledge with veterans so they can use it to improve their lives and those of their families. Regardless of which direction you choose to take your life, I encourage you to realize your full potential and to use it in a positive way moving forward.

Life is extremely difficult, and trusting people can be even more difficult. It takes us all growing and learning together to prosper. Many other books have been designed to help veterans, and there are many places to gather information to develop your plans further. I encourage you to seek some of those resources as needed. I have three last points to share with you that I hope will be a lamp to your feet, no matter the path you choose.

1. Find Your Passion

You know yourself better than anyone else. You know better than your spouse, parents, or friends what you like and do not like. You know what will motivate you, and you also know what can bring you down. When you are true to yourself and you focus your energy on the positives of life and the good you have to offer this world, then you will find your passion— that thing that will make you happy. It may not come easily;

you will likely have to make sacrifices and go through some dark days. When that happens, remember you are not alone; there are people in this world who want you to succeed in more ways than one. Be true to yourself and your passion, and you will succeed.

> *Have the patience to see your plan through and the trust to know it will happen, and a definitive light will appear at the end of the tunnel.*

2. Stay Dedicated

Life is not always fair. Tragedy can and will happen as part of life. You have to stay vigilant during these times. You have to stay focused and not allow adversity to defeat you. Realize that many things happen that are outside your control, but do your best to persevere anyway. Understanding that you are a good person and that, as a leader, you can turn a negative situation into a positive one will make all the difference.

Having the ability to push forward is the only element that separates those who are successful from those who are not. Success is measured not only in terms of dollars and cents but also in the value system that guides you as you work to help yourself and others. When you stay true to yourself and are committed to the task at hand, good things will happen. They may not be today, but they will happen. You just have to keep the faith in yourself that you are doing everything it takes to beat the odds.

> *Knowing how to adapt and overcome is not only a military strategy but also a life strategy.*

3. Keep Climbing

There are many different paths in life. No matter what path you are on, there is always another path up ahead waiting for you. Are you prepared both to complete the journey you are currently on and to take the road that awaits you ahead? Most likely you are not because it is almost impossible to be prepared for every situation that will occur in life. When we reach these crossroads, we must remember we are stronger than what we think and that we are not alone in our struggles to overcome adversity.

That is why it is very important to "ruck up" and keep climbing, no matter the obstacle in your way. Only you have the power and control to make the difference you want in this world. You must keep fighting, climbing, and surviving without losing sight of where you have come from and where you are going. The destination is not far away, and you are heading in the right direction, so choose to fight on instead of abandoning ship.

> *There is a purpose for everyone in this world, and yours starts with your resiliency never to quit.*

Conclusion

Looking back over the course of my life, I have come to realize that if I had had the guidance of a mentor or confidante, I might have not made certain decisions that hurt me or set me back. From the time I got out of the military to now, I have probably made hundreds of bad decisions while also making some good ones. Good or bad, those decisions shaped me into who I am today, and they have made me stronger in more ways than one. However, I would probably be in a better place or further along in my maturity process if I'd had someone there to guide me toward personal and professional goals that would have enhanced my knowledge, skills, and abilities in this world sooner rather than later.

Whether you are just leaving the military or have already done so, this book provides a solid foundation you can expand upon. Having the perspective of another veteran, soldier, and/or professional sure makes the transition from military to civilian that much easier. The chapters and suggestions outlined in this book were geared toward positive strategies that allow your mind to think outside the box to reach your dreams, no matter the obstacles in your way.

Sometimes, you just have to go for it. You have to put it all on the line and take some calculated risks to determine whether a course of action is the right one for you. The main goal is to narrow down your decision-making process to identify a clear strategy for your success. The ball is now in your court.

Will you delay, or will you start planning for your future now? The small steps are what make up the large advancements in life. It took meeting the right veteran, who saw the value in me, for me to see value in myself. Having the vision and direction to move forward consistently will make all the difference for a veteran struggling to be on a solid footing. I hope I have given you that vision so you can stand on your own two feet with extreme confidence, and even if you may fall at some point, you will be able to get back up and be even stronger than before!

May you enjoy much success!

Acknowledgments

I wish to thank Allen Allison, US Army veteran, for changing my life. He took me under his wing, despite the fact that I was broken. He helped me to believe in myself and see the man I could be. He was the one person who saw the good in me and realized that, with the right amount of guidance, I could use my gifts from God to help those around me.

My children, Ariel and Zachary, have been very brave and strong supporting me while I ventured out to help make the world a better place. Their sacrifice allows me to gain the necessary tools to shape the future I strive for; then they will ultimately have the ability to succeed without sacrificing the way I have during their own lives. They are the breath I take on a daily basis and without them I would be completely lost.

Thank you to everyone who has supported me and who has truly believed in me. Coming from the bottom and going to the top is quite difficult without adequate resources at your disposal. However, the right people have always come into my life at the right moment to help me get to the next milepost on my journey, and for that, I am eternally grateful to God, our Father in Heaven. Life is not easy, but with faith, hope, and love, we all can reach our destinations.

Veterans Resource List

Appeals, http://www.warms.vba.va.gov/admin21/m21_1/mr/part1/ch05.doc

Board of Veterans Appeals, http://www.va.gov/vbs/bva/

CARES Commission, http://www.va.gov/vbs/bva/

CARES Draft National Plan, http://www1.va.gov/cares/page.cfm?pg=105

Center for Minority Veterans, http://www1.va.gov/centerforminorityveterans/

Center for Veterans Enterprise, http://www.vetbiz.gov/default2.htm

Center for Women Veterans, http://www1.va.gov/womenvet/

Clarification on the changes in VA healthcare for Gulf War Veterans http://www.gulfwarvets.com/ubb/Forum1/HTML/000016.html

Classified Records—American Gulf War Veterans Association, http://www.gulfwarvets.com/ubb/Forum18/HTML/000011.html

Compensation for Disabilities Associated with the Gulf War Service, http://www.warms.vba.va.gov/admin21/m21_1/part6%20/ch07.doc

Compensation Rate Tables, 12-1-03, http://www.vba.va.gov/bln/21/Rates/comp01.htm

Department of Veterans Affairs, http://www.va.gov/

Department of Veterans Affairs PTSD: National Center for PTSD, http://www.ptsd.va.gov

Directory of Veterans Service Organizations, http://www1.va.gov/vso/index.cfm?template=view

Due Process, http://www.warms.vba.va.gov/admin21/m21_1/mr/part1/ch02.doc

Duty to Assist, http://www.warms.vba.va.gov/admin21/m21_1/mr/part1/ch01.doc

Electronic Code of Federal Regulations, http://www.gpoaccess.gov/ecfr/

Emergency, Non-Emergency, and Fee Basis Care, http://www1.va.gov/opa/vadocs/fedben.pdf

Environmental Agents, http://www1.va.gov/environagents/

Environmental Agents M10, http://www1.va.gov/vhapublications/View-Publication.asp?pub_ID=1002

Establishing Combat Veteran Eligibility, http://www1.va.gov/vhapublications/ViewPublication.asp?pub_ID=315

Evaluation Protocol for Gulf War and Iraqi Freedom Veterans with Potential Exposure to Depleted Uranium (Du), http://www1.va.gov/gulfwar/docs/DUHandbook1303122304.DOC http://www1.va.gov/vhapublications/ViewPublication.asp?pub_ID=1158 See also, Depleted Uranium Fact Sheet, http://www1.va.gov/gulfwar/docs/DepletedUraniumFAQSheet.doc

Evaluation Protocol for Non-Gulf War Veterans with Potential Exposure to Depleted Uranium (Du), http://www1.va.gov/gulfwar/docs/DU-HANDBOOKNONGW130340304.DOC

Fee Basis, Priority for Outpatient Medical Services and Inpatient Hospital Care, http://www1.va..gov/vhapublications/ViewPublication.asp?pub_ID=206

Federal Benefits for Veterans and Dependants 2005, http://www1.va.gov/opa/vadocs/fedben.pdf or http://www1.va..gov/opa/vadocs/current_benefits.htm

Forms and Records Request, http://www.va.gov/vaforms/

General Compensation Provisions, http://www.access.gpo.gov/uscode/title38/partii_chapter11_subchaptervi_.html

Geriatrics and Extended Care, http://www1.va.gov/geriatricsshg/

GI Bill, http://www.gibill.va.gov/

Guideline for Chronic Pain and Fatigue MUS-CPG, http://www.oqp.med.va.gov/cpg/cpgn/mus/mus_base.htm

Guide to Gulf War Veteran's Health, http://www1.va.gov/gulfwar/docs/VHIgulfwar.pdf

Gulf War Subject Index, http://www1.va.gov/GulfWar/page.cfm?pg=7&-template=main&letter=A

Gulf War Veterans' Illnesses Q&As, http://www1.va.gov/gulfwar/docs/GWIllnessesQandAsIB1041.pdf

Hearings, http://www.warms.vba.va.gov/admin21/m21_1/mr/part1/ch04.doc

Homeless Veterans, http://www1.va.gov/homeless/

HSR&D (Health Services Research & Development), http://www.hsrd. research.va.gov/

Index to Disability Examination Worksheets C&P Exams, http://www. vba.va.gov/bln/21/benefits/exams/index.htm

Ionizing Radiation, http://www1.va.gov/irad/

Iraqi Freedom/Enduring Freedom Veterans VBA, http://www.vba. va.gov/EFIF/

M21-1 Table of Contents, http://www.warms.vba.va.gov/M21_1.html

Mental Disorders, Schedule of Ratings, http://www.warms.vba.va.gov/ regs/38CFR/BOOKC/PART4/S4_130.DOC

Mental Health Program Guidelines, http://www1.va.gov/vhapublica-tions/ViewPublication.asp?pub_ID=1094

Mental Illness Research, Education, and Clinical Centers, http://www. mirecc.med.va.gov/

MS (Multiple Sclerosis) Centers of Excellence, http://www.va.gov/ms/ about.asp

My Health eVet, http://www.myhealth.va.gov/

NASDVA (National Association of State Directors of Veterans Affairs), http://nasdva.com/

National Center for Health Promotion and Disease Prevention, http:// www.nchpdp.med.va.gov/postdeploymentlinks.asp

Neurological Conditions and Convulsive Disorders, Schedule of Ratings, http://www.warms.vba.va.gov/regs/38cfr/bookc/part4/s4%5F124a. doc

OMI (Office of Medical Inspector), http://www.omi.cio.med.va.gov/

Online VA Form 10-10EZ, https://www.1010ez..med.va.gov/sec/ vha/1010ez/

Parkinson's Disease and Related Neurodegenerative Disorders, http:// www1.va.gov/resdev/funding/solicitations/docs/parkinsons.pdf http://www1.va.gov/padrecc/

Peacetime Disability Compensation, http://frwebgate.access.gpo.gov/cgi-bin/getdoc.cgi?dbname=browse_usc&docid=Cite:+38USC1131

Persian Gulf Registry, http://www1.va.gov/vhapublications/ViewPublica-tion.asp?pub_ID=1003
This program is now referred to as Gulf War Registry Program (to include Operation Iraqi Freedom) as of March 7, 2005, http:// www1..va.gov/vhapublications/ViewPublication.asp?pub_ID=1232

Persian Gulf Registry Referral Centers, http://www1.va.gov/vhapublications/ViewPublication.asp?pub_ID=1006

Persian Gulf Veterans' Illnesses Research 1999, Annual Report to Congress, http://www1.va.gov/resdev/1999_Gulf_War_Veterans'_Illnesses_Appendices.doc

Persian Gulf Veterans' Illnesses Research 2002, Annual Report to Congress, http://www1.va.gov/resdev/prt/gulf_war_2002/GulfWarRpt02.pdf

Power of Attorney, http://www.warms.vba..va.gov/admin21/m21_1/mr/part1/ch03.doc

Project 112 (Including Project SHAD), http://www1.va.gov/shad/

Prosthetics Eligibility, http://www1.va.gov/vhapublications/ViewPublication.asp?pub_ID=337

Public Health and Environmental Hazards, http://www.vethealth.cio.med.va.gov/

Public Health/SARS, http://www..publichealth.va.gov/SARS/

Publications and Reports, http://www1.va.gov/resdev/prt/pubs_individual.cfm?webpage=gulf_war.htm

Publications Manuals, http://www1.va.gov/vhapublications/publications.cfm?Pub=4

Records Center and Vault, http://www.aac.va.gov/vault/default.html

Records Center and Vault Site Map, http://www.aac.va.gov/vault/sitemap.html

Request for and Consent to Release of Information from Claimant's Records, http://www.forms.va.gov/va/Internet/VARF/getformharness.asp?formName=3288-form.xft

Research Advisory Committee on Gulf War Veterans' Illnesses, http://www1.va.gov/rac-gwvi/docs/ReportandRecommendations_2004.pdf

Research Advisory Committee on Gulf War Veterans' Illnesses April 11, 2002, http://www1.va.gov/rac-gwvi/docs/Minutes_April112002.doc

Research and Development, http://www.appc1.va.gov/resdev/programs/all_programs.cfm

Survivors and Dependents' Educational Assistance, http://www.access.gpo.gov/uscode/title38/partiii_chapter35_.html

Title 38 Index Parts 0-17,
http://ecfr.gpoaccess.gov/cgi/t/text/text-idx?sid=1b0c269b510d-3157fbf8f8801bc9b3dc&c=ecfr&tpl=/ecfrbrowse/Title38/38c-frv1_02.tpl

Title 38 Part 4—Schedule for Rating Disabilities Subpart B—Disability Ratings, http://ecfr.gpoaccess.gov/cgi/t/text/text-idx?c=ecfr&sid=ab7641af-d195c84a49a2067dbbcf95c0&rgn=div6&view=tex-t&node=38:1.0.1.1.5.2&idno=38

Title 38 Part 4.16 Total Disability Ratings for Compensation Based on Unemployability of the Individual; General Policy in Rating, http://www.ecfr.gov/cgi-bin/text-idx-?rgn=div6;node=38%3A1.0.1.1.5.1

Title 38 Part 18, http://ecfr.gpoaccess.gov/cgi/t/text/text-idx?sid=1b-0c269b510d3157fbf8f8801bc9b3dc&c=ecfr&tpl=/ecfrbrowse/Ti-tle38/38cfrv2_02.tpl

Title 38 CFR Part 3, Subpart A - Pension, Compensation, and Dependency and Indemnity Compensation, http://www.ecfr.gov/cgi-bin/text-idx?tpl=/ecfrbrowse/Title38/38c-fr3_main_02.tpl

Title 38 Pensions, Bonuses & Veterans Relief (also 3.317 Compensation for certain disabilities due to undiagnosed illnesses found here), http://ecfr.gpoaccess.gov/cgi/t/text/text-idx?c=ecfr&sid=1b-0c269b510d3157fbf8f8801bc9b3dc&tpl=/ecfrbrowse/Title38/38c-fr3_main_02.tpl

US Court of Appeals for Veterans Claims, http://www.vetapp.gov/

VA Best Practice Manual for Posttraumatic Stress Disorder (PTSD), http://www.avapl.org/pub/PTSD%20Manual%20final%206.pdf

VA Fact Sheet, http://www1.va.gov/opa/fact/gwfs.html

VA Health Care Eligibility, http://www.va.gov/healtheligibility/home/hecmain.asp

VA Instituting Global Assessment of Function (GAF), http://www.avapl.org/gaf/gaf.html

VA Life Insurance Handbook, Chapter 3, http://www.insurance.va.gov/inForceGliSite/GLIhandbook/glibookletch3.htm#310

VA Loan Lending Limits and Jumbo Loans, http://valoans.com/va_facts_limits.cfm

VA MS Research, http://www.va.gov/ms/about.asp

VA National Hepatitis C Program, http://www.hepatitis.va.gov/

VA Office of Research and Development, http://www1.va.gov/resdev/

VA OIG Hotline Telephone Number and Address, http://www.va..gov/oig/hotline/hotline3.htm

VA Trainee Pocket Card on Gulf War, http://www.va.gov/OAA/pocket-card/gulfwar.asp

VA WMD EMSHG, http://www1.va.gov/emshg/

VA WRIISC-DC, http://www.va.gov/WRIISC-DC/

Vet Center Eligibility—Readjustment Counseling Service, http://www.va.gov/rcs/Eligibility.htm

Veterans Benefits Administration, http://www.vba.va.gov/

Veterans Legal and Benefits Information, http://valaw.org/

VHA Forms, Publications, Manuals, http://www1.va.gov/vhapublications/

VHA Programs—Clinical Programs & Initiatives, http://www.va.gov/health/orgs.asp

VHA Public Health Strategic Health Care Group, http://www.publichealth.va.gov/

VHI Guide to Gulf War Veterans Health, http://www1.va.gov/vhi_ind_study/gulfwar/istudy/index.asp

Vocational Rehabilitation http://www.vba.va.gov/bln/vre/

Vocational Rehabilitation Subsistence, http://www.vba.va.gov/bln/vre/InterSubsistencefy04.doc

VONAPP, http://vabenefits.vba.va.gov/vonapp/main.asp

WARMS - 38 CFR Book C, http://www.warms.vba.va.gov/bookc.html

War-Related Illness and Injury Study Center—New Jersey, http://www.wri.med.va.gov/

Wartime Disability Compensation, http://frwebgate.access.gpo.gov/cgi-bin/getdoc.cgi?dbname=browse_usc&docid=Cite:+38USC1110

What VA Social Workers Do, http://www1.va.gov/socialwork/page.cfm?pg=3

WRIISC Patient Eligibility, http://www.illegion.org/va1.html

About the Author

Michael Bluemling Jr. has overcome the abuse of his past to achieve a fulfilling life. After high school, he served in the United States Army, obtaining the rank of sergeant. He received the US Army Commendation Medal and two US Army Achievement Medals, the US Army Good Conduct Medal, the Kosovo Campaign Medal, and the NATO Medal. After an honorable discharge from the military, he held various positions in the US Department of Labor and at the Department of Veteran Affairs.

Michael holds a bachelor of science degree in business administration from ECPI University, a master of professional studies in human resources and employment relations from Pennsylvania State University, and a graduate certificate from UMass Dartmouth in Organizational Leadership.

The trauma of his past has led Michael to making a difference for others in the present. He is the founder of Power of One, a disabled-veteran–owned company based in Richmond, Virginia. Power of One is centered on meeting the needs of its customers by providing dynamic inspirational presentations that allow for personal growth and life fulfillment. A critical element of the company's vision is to help others and give back to the local community. Michael and the company were highlighted in *U.S. Veterans Magazine* in November 2013 and *Disabled American Veterans Magazine* in the July/August 2014 issues.

To promote his message that each person has the power to deal with adversity and move forward, no matter the circumstances, Michael has written *Turning the Page: Overcoming Abuse to Reach Life's Fulfillment*, *Our Journey: Heart to Heart with God*, and now *Bridging the Gap from Soldier to Civilian: A Road Map to Success for Veterans*.

To learn more about Michael Bluemling Jr. and his organization, visit:

www.PowerofOneLLC.com